Success
with
Oils

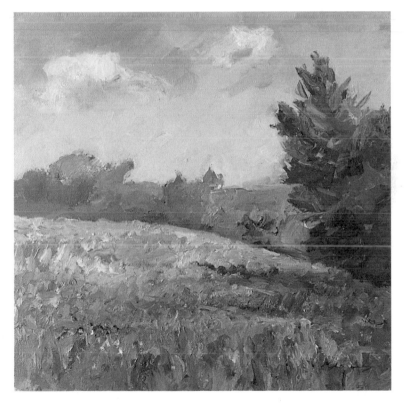

WATSON-GUPTILL PUBLICATIONS/NEW YORK

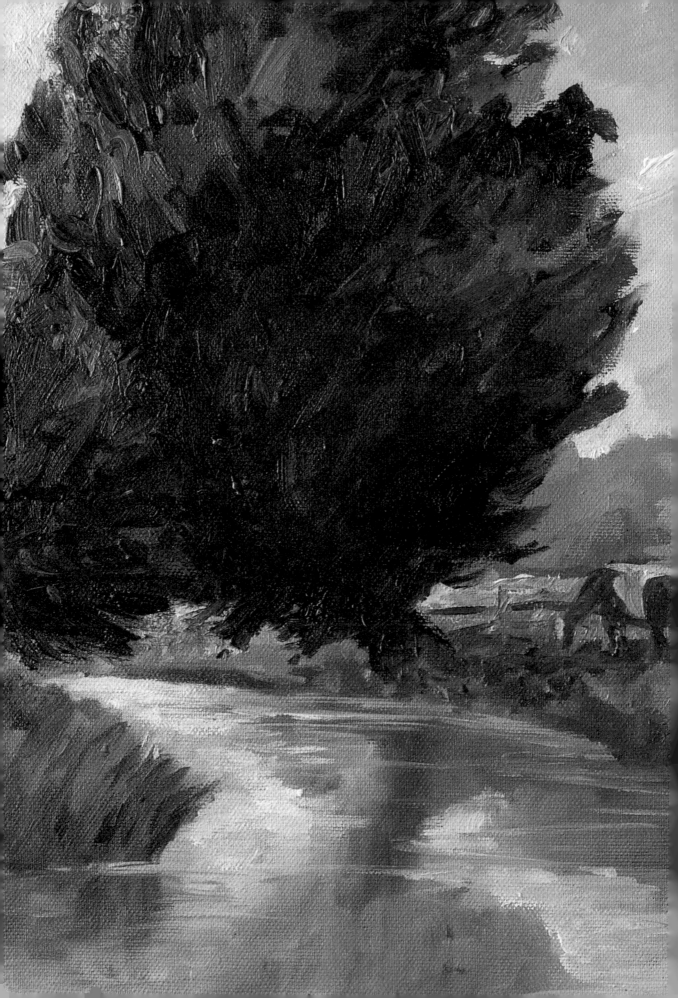

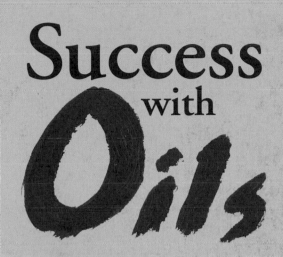

Success
with
Oils

Melanie
Cambridge

WATSON-GUPTILL PUBLICATIONS/NEW YORK

ACKNOWLEDGEMENTS

My thanks to Geoffrey Frankcom for encouraging me to write this book in the first place and to Cathy Gosling at HarperCollins for having confidence in me. Thanks also to Caroline Churton, Geraldine Christy, Julie Francis, and Laura Knox for helping me through the production process. Finally, my grateful thanks to my husband, Peter, for his belief in me and constant encouragement over the years.

First published in the US in 2003 by
Watson-Guptill Publications
A division of VNU Business Media, Inc.
770 Broadway, New York, NY10003
www.watsonguptill.com

First published in the UK in 2002 by
Collins, an imprint of
HarperCollins*Publishers*
77-85 Fulham Palace Road
Hammersmith, London W6 8JB

Library of Congress Control number:
2002109817

ISBN: 0 8230 4941 8

Editor: Geraldine Christy
Designer: Julie Francis
Photographer: Laura Knox

Printed and bound by Bath Press Colour Books

1 2 3 4 5 6 7 8 / 08 07 06 05 04 03

PAGE 1: High Summer, 16 x 16 in (41 x 41 cm)
PAGES 2-3: Evening Light, River Wey 12 x 20 in (31 x 51 cm)
PAGES 4-5: Towards San Gimignano 10 x 8 in (25 x 20 cm)

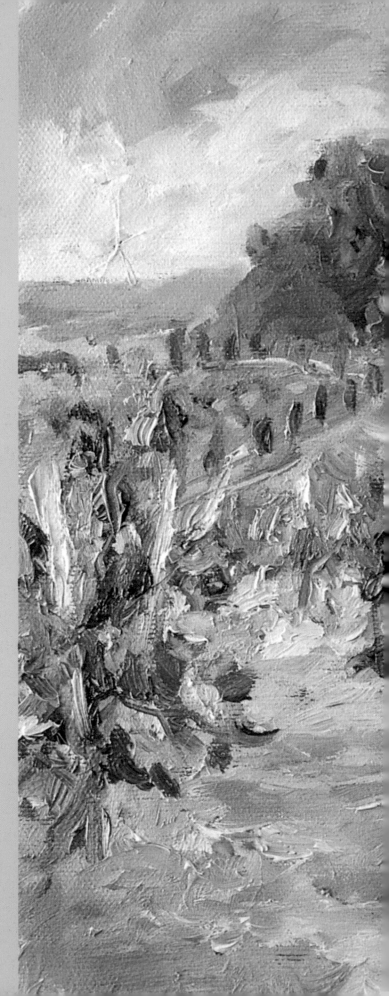

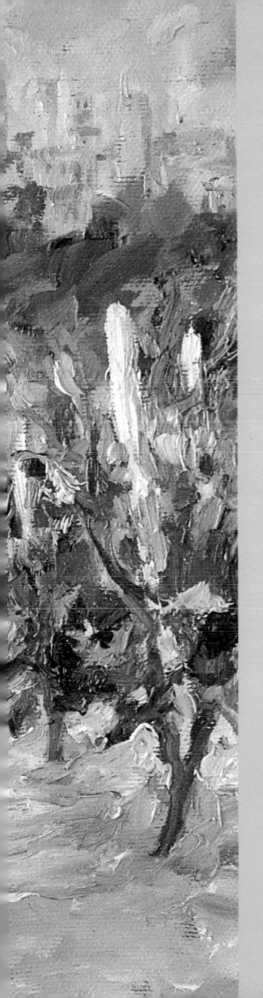

Contents

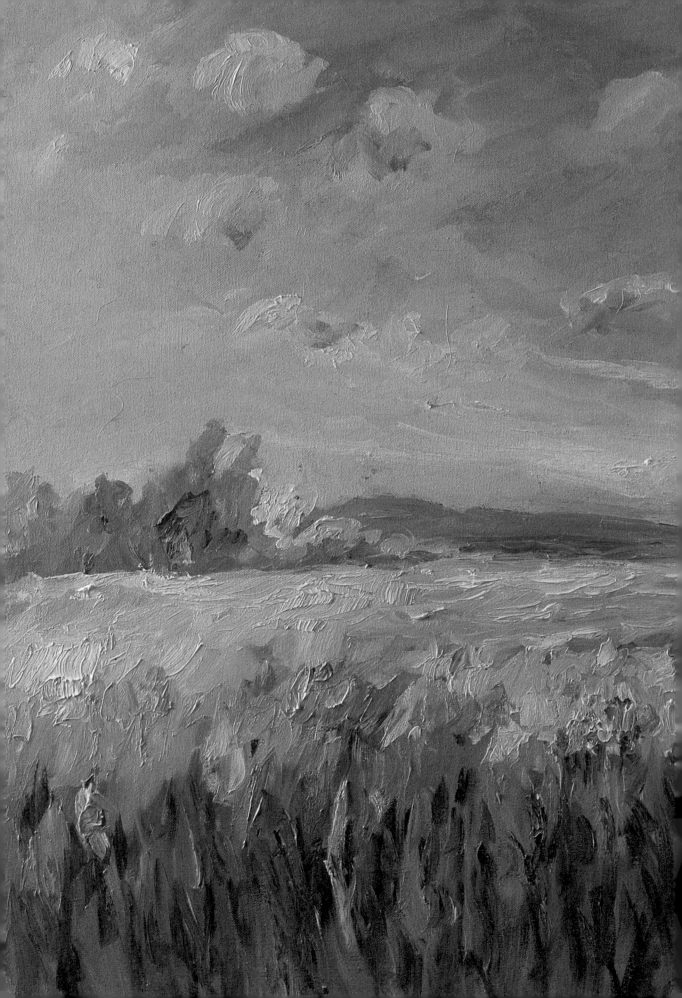

Introduction

I love painting in oils, particularly for landscapes. Oil paints seem to lend themselves to landscape subjects, having both the subtlety to depict a misty river and the vibrancy to capture the dazzling colors of the Mediterranean. The pleasure of squeezing all that color onto a dark mahogany palette always sparks off feelings of excitement and anticipation. I find even the buttery texture of the paint alluring.

◀ **Hay Fever**
20 x 36 in (51 x 91 cm)

ABOUT THIS BOOK

For you who wish to try oils for the first time, this book offers a simplified approach to help you get started. Throughout the book, examples show you how to create successful oil paintings in only one session. A variety of landscape subjects is presented, helping you to gain confidence when painting from sketches, photographs, or on the site itself. While sketches are important for gathering material and ideas, the ability to draw well is not essential for success. Many of the examples in this book are painted directly from rough, annotated sketches with no detailed foundation drawing on the canvas at all

Each chapter introduces a specific technique or subject. More experienced students can look at the elements of most interest to them. For example, bringing paintings to life with figures is an area that many students find difficul

I have tried to dispel the myths that oils are difficult and messy and require great deal of materials and space. I suggest a minimum of equipment, gel mediums, and brush cleaners, all of

▼ **The Old Church, Send**
12 x 16 in (30 x 41 cm)
This painting was produced on site in the late afternoon. The church was painted very loosely with a minimum of detail. I worked quickly with a No. 8 flat brush to create the rough meadow in the foreground. Notice how the addition of alizarin crimson warms this area, helping to bring the scene forward visually.

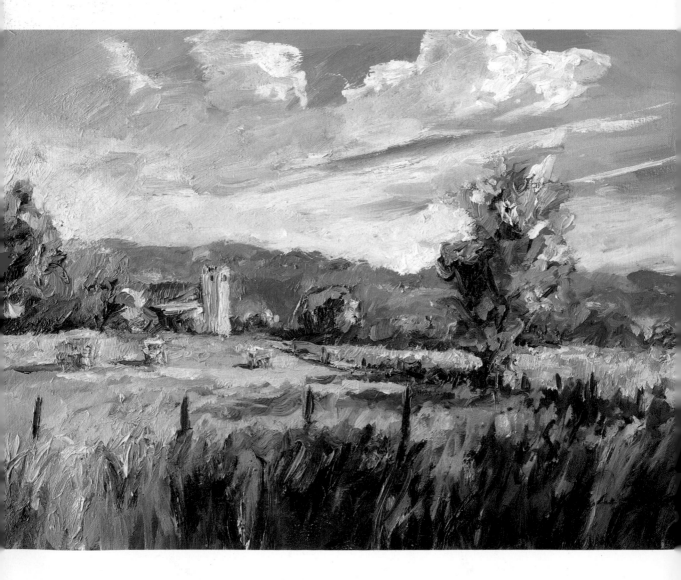

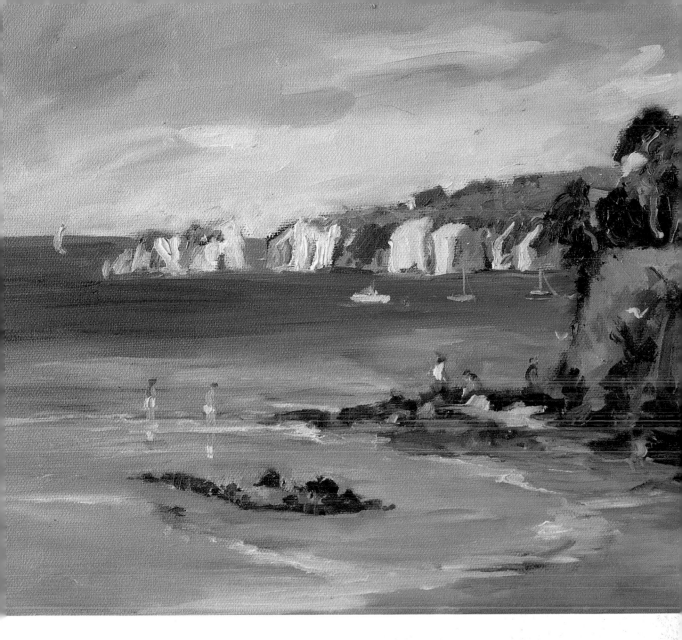

...hich will enable you to work
...omfortably indoors without any of
...ne usual associated fumes and other
...xpected drawbacks.

Most sections of this book are
...ccompanied by a step-by-step
...emonstration, since it has been my
...xperience that people learn first of
...ll by copying. These demonstrtions
...ke you through each stage of the
...ainting so that you can fully
...nderstand how the painting develops
...om the initial idea to the finished
...ork. Details are included alongside

certain stages to highlight a particular
technique or point of interest. You will
also find various short exercises to follow.
Again, these are there to help you as a
beginner – I hope you will find them fun
to do as well as helpful for understanding
a particular technique.

I have also added Tips boxes which are
designed to draw your attention to points
about working methods and to offer
simple solutions to everyday painting
problems. Since I cannot be with you at
each stage, I hope you will find my
comments and suggestions useful.

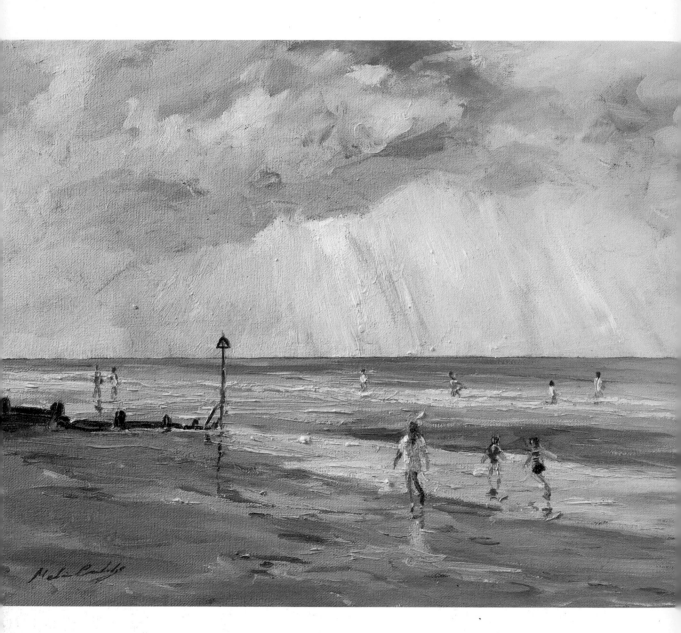

▲ **Low Tide at Camber Sands**
11 x 14 in (28 x 36 cm)
The key to this painting is its atmospheric sky. The figures as they played in the tidal pools were captured with just a few brushstrokes.

OILS – A FORGIVING MEDIUM

The real magic of oil paints comes from their versatility. In the last two centuries artists have used oils in all sorts of different painting styles to create works of art, from the almost photographic qualities produced by painters such as the Pre-Raphaelites, to the looser work of the Impressionists, and on to Cubism and other forms of abstraction. There is also a range of textures possible with oil paints. Oils can be thinned to a wash-like consistency, blended to a smooth finish, or applied very thickly and roughly, leaving the brushmarks clearly visible. Indeed, the brushmark is probably as important an element in contemporary oil painting as the color used. This emphasis on individual brushstrokes in oil painting makes it much easier for the beginner. Solid strokes can be used to 'build' a figure, a boat, or house without drawin an initial outline. Look at how Paul Cézanne (1839–1906) experimented with brushstrokes, using them to create shapes in blocks of color.

Some ability to draw is important for any kind of painting style; but drawing, by its very nature, is based on the use of line. In a painting, however, the line is not always the most important factor. More essential, perhaps, is the ability to 'see' areas of color and tone and learning how to place theses elements on the canvas appropriately to 'build' a finished painting. Throughout this book I have tried to teach you how to create a painting by 'building.' Because oil painting is basically an opaque medium,

it is ideal for use in this way. Large areas of solid color can be established at the very beginning of the painting process to create the overall composition, with details added in later stages. Since oil paints dry very slowly, however, – over several days or more – there is plenty of time to alter an oil painting or even to scrape off a painted area and start again. This takes away some of the pressure of getting everything right first time – a great advantage for the beginner and more experienced artist alike!

With such a forgiving and exciting medium, oil painting offers so much to the beginner – so what are you waiting for? Go ahead and start!

▼ **Dusk**
12 x 20 in (31 x 51 cm)
Note how the brushstrokes themselves create the textures and shapes of the main tree as well as the flower heads in the darkening meadow. I did almost no pre-drawing, concentrating instead on the way the colors and tones relate to each other.

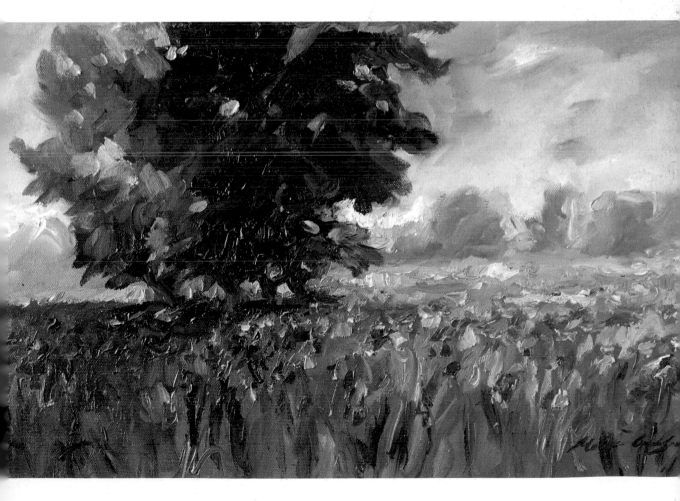

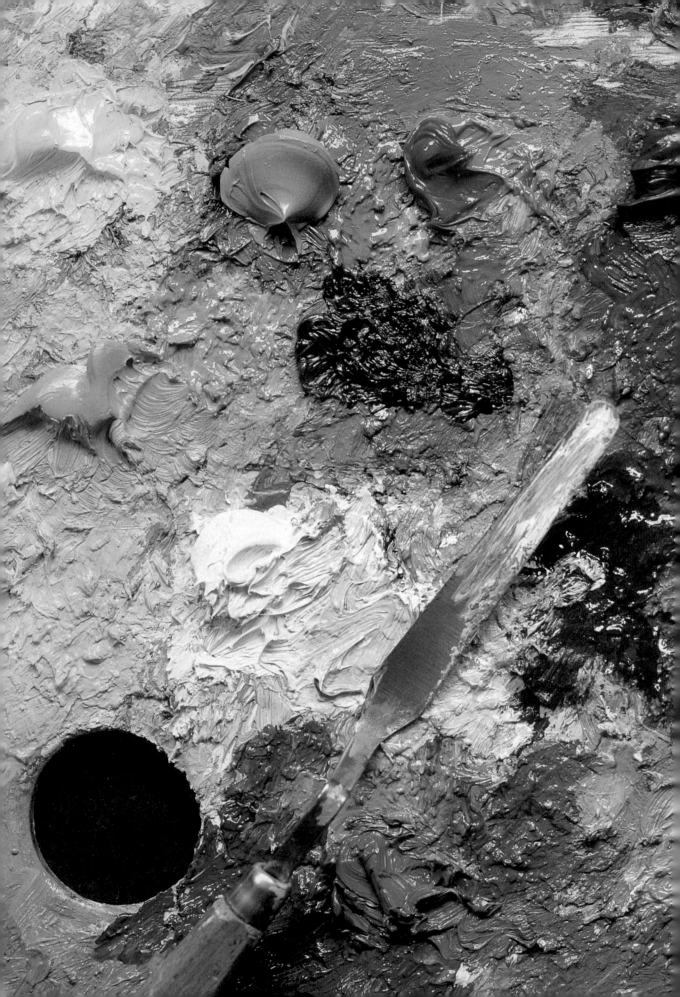

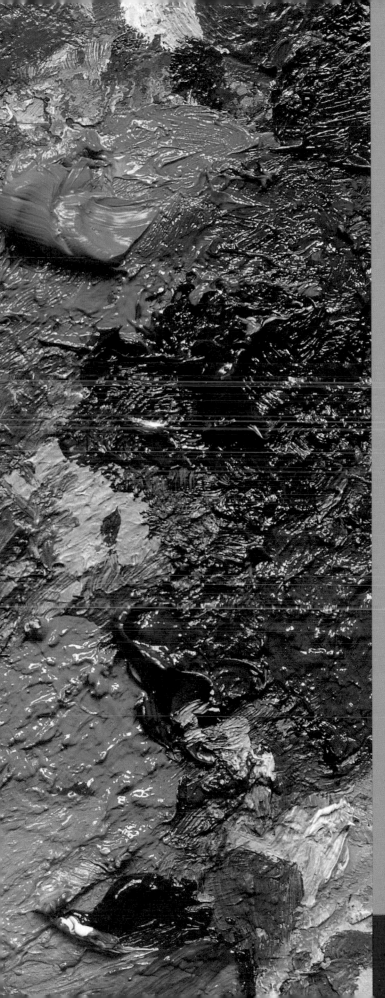

Materials and Equipment

The beginner artist faces a bewildering amount of equipment on visiting an art supply store. Add to this the false idea that oils are "smelly" and "difficult," that they require special thinners such as turpentine, linseed oil, and stand oil, it's no wonder that the beginner is put off! But actually, all a person needs to get started are a few colors, three or four brushes, and an odorless gel for thinning the paints.

◀ Melanie's working palette loaded with fresh paint.

COLORS

Oil paint comes in tubes and is normally available in two different grades: artist quality and student quality. Artist grade pigments are slightly more expensive, but the difference in quality is considerable. Since you will only be working with a few colors, these are well worth the extra cost. Tubes of varying sizes are available. Tubes containing 38 ml are a suitable size to begin with, but do invest in a larger tube of titanium white, say 60 ml. Unlike watercolors, oils are an opaque medium and need the addition of white to create the paler tints. Thus you will tend to use much more white pigment in proportion to any of the other colors.

As well as traditional oils, there are also various "special oils" on the market, including water-soluable oils and alkyd paints, which are faster drying.

The basic palette

You need only a basic palette of eight colors, plus white, to begin. This should comprise two blues, two yellows, two oranges, one red, and one green.

The blues I suggest are French ultramarine and cerulean. Choose lemon yellow and raw sienna for your two yellows. The orange shades I suggest are cadmium orange and light red. Alizarin crimson is a useful red, and viridian makes a good basic green. These eight colors will allow you to mix all the colors you will need for landscape painting.

I also recommend titanium white since it is a very bright, opaque white.

I do not use black. Having it available on the palette makes it tempting to darken a color by simply adding black, but this can make colors dull and lifeless. Instead, try mixing French ultramarine and light red for your darkest tones.

▼ **Basic color palette**

French Ultramarine
A deep warm blue and a good all-round color.

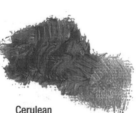

Cerulean
A cold turquoise blue, useful for skies and making wonderful grays.

Lemon Yellow
A cold bright yellow, excellent for mixing spring greens.

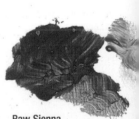

Raw Sienna
A warm earthy yellow, useful for producing warm greens and browns.

Cadmium Orange
A bright orange for mixing warm grays and cloud tones.

Light Red
A brownish orange for making dark tones and greens.

Alizarin Crimson
A dark red that produces strong purples and dark greens.

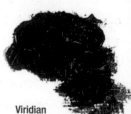

Viridian
A very strong green, excellent for mixing, but not for use on its own.

These two colors make very lively darks and are far preferable to black for landscape painting.

Additional colors

Once you begin to feel confident working with the basic palette of eight colors, you may wish to add a few more. The following colors are the ones I find to be useful additions from time to time: naples yellow, cadmium yellow deep, rose madder, raw umber, cobalt blue, and sap green.

BRUSHES

Brushes for oil painting are traditionally made from hog hair. There are a number of excellent synthetic brushes on the market, however. Rather than have a large number of brushes, start off with four or five, along with a palette knife for mixing colors on the palette and occasionally scraping paint off the canvas).

I recommend that you start with five brushes. A No. 10 (1 in or 25 mm) short flat nylon brush is ideal for blocking in large areas of color for establishing the main structure of the painting. A No. 8 (⅝ in or 16 mm) short flat nylon brush is my most useful brush because it is both capable of blocking in medium areas of color and useful for moderate detail work. A smaller No. 4 (⅜ in or 10 mm) short flat nylon is used for details and basic shapes like buildings. I also use two round nylon brushes: a No. 4 round as a basic fine detail brush, and a No. 4 rigger, ideal for painting branches and very fine lines.

▼ **Additional colors**

Naples Yellow
A warm cream tone.

Cadmium Yellow Deep
A bright orange yellow useful for painting sunflowers and cornfields.

Rose Madder
A deep pink that gives warmer purples and grays.

Raw Umber
A soft brown.

Cobalt Blue
A bright blue, makes a useful addition for skies.

Sap Green
A warm olive green shade.

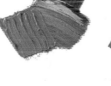

▼ Five brushes are all you need to start with.

No.10 short flat nylon
(1 in or 25 mm)

No. 0 short flat nylon
(⅝ in or 16 mm)

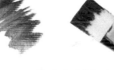

No. 4 short flat nylon
(⅜ in or 10 mm)

No. 4 round nylon

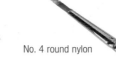

No. 4 nylon rigger

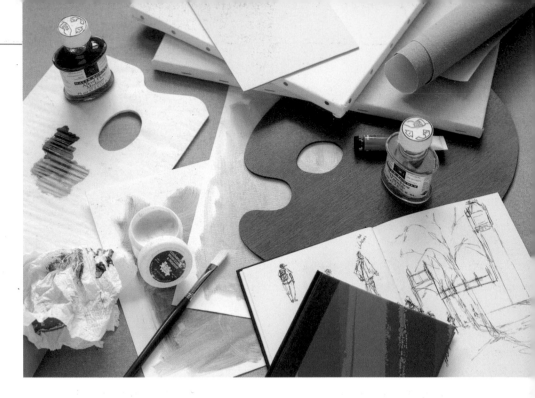

▶ A selection of painting surfaces and other basic materials.

PAINTING SURFACES

Oil paints can be used on a number of different surfaces. The traditional surface is stretched cotton or linen canvas, but canvas boards and oil sketching paper are acceptable alternatives and are less expensive. Pieces of matt board or even cardboard can make useful surfaces for a quick sketch, although they are not ideal for a full painting.

It is possible to buy canvases pre-primed and stretched onto a frame. These come packaged with a set of wedges. Knock each wedge into the corner of the canvas at the back to tighten up the surface until it is "drum tight" and it's ready for painting. Canvas boards also make good supports for finished paintings since they are less expensive than a stretched panel while still providing a woven textured surface.

MEDIUMS AND THINNERS

Traditionally, oils are used in combination with a number of highly toxic mediums and thinners, including turpentine, linseed oil, and stand oil. For simplicity, however, and to avoid the fumes associated with these products, I use an alkyd gel medium. Alkyd mediums are generally odorless making them ideal for use indoors. They also speed up the drying process, cutting it almost in half, so that even traditional oils are touch-dry in three to four hours.

For cleaning brushes, try using kerosene. It is less harmful than turpentine and has a less pronounced smell. Remember to keep a lid on the kerosene while working, however, to avoid inhaling fumes. It is possible now to use a special soap cleaner or brush-restorer to clean brushes. A more expensive option than thinners, it works well and is especially useful when painting out of doors.

Keep plenty of rags handy to wipe off excess paint from the brushes as you go along, rather than cleaning your brush completely every time you change col

PALETTES

Palettes, made of wood or plastic, come in many sizes, and are normally kidney shaped or oblong. Experiment to find one that has enough space for mixing colors but not too heavy to hold in one hand. It is also possible to use a sheet of glass or disposable palette sheets.

Most of the exercises in this book are produced on an earth-colored ground rather than white canvas. The color of a wooden palette is similar to the colored canvas, so for this reason I recommend a wooden rather than a plastic palette to begin with. This makes it easier for you to match the colors visually.

EASELS

When painting with oils it is preferable to have the canvas fairly upright. The easiest way to achieve this is by using an easel. You can use either a simple wooden sketching easel or a full-sized

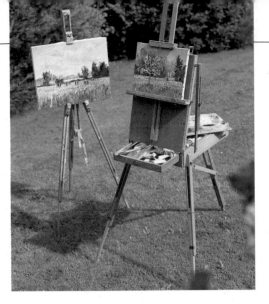

◀ A portable easel keeps the canvas in an upright position and enables you to stand back from the painting while working. Finished oil paintings are generally viewed from about 2 m (6 ft) away, so it is helpful to be able to take a step back from your work to see how it will appear when seen from this distance.

studio one. If studio space is at a premium, a box easel may be the answer because it will both hold all your equipment and fold away for storage. However, a full-sized box easel weighs around 6 lb (3 kg) empty and even more when filled with tubes of paint, etc.

WORKING OUTDOORS

If you intend to paint mainly outdoors a pochade box makes a useful addition to your equipment. I would not suggest one as a replacement for an easel, but it is ideal for working outside, allowing you to work relatively unobserved by passers-by. It can even be used sitting in the car.

▼ A pochade box incorporates a small pull-out palette and tubes of paint and brushes; there is space in its lid for two or three small canvas boards, often only 7 x 5 in (18 x 13 cm) to 10 x 8 in (25 x 20 cm) in size at most.

to sum up

Oil painting equipment can be kept to a minimum. To start off you will need:

8 oil colors, plus white
5 brushes
1 palette knife
wooden palette
single dipper (clips onto the palette to hold gel medium)
gel medium
can of kerosene or can of soap brush cleaner
plenty of rags
a suitable easel or table stand

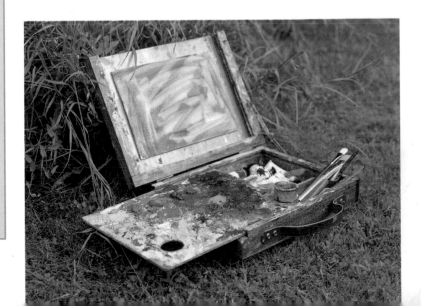

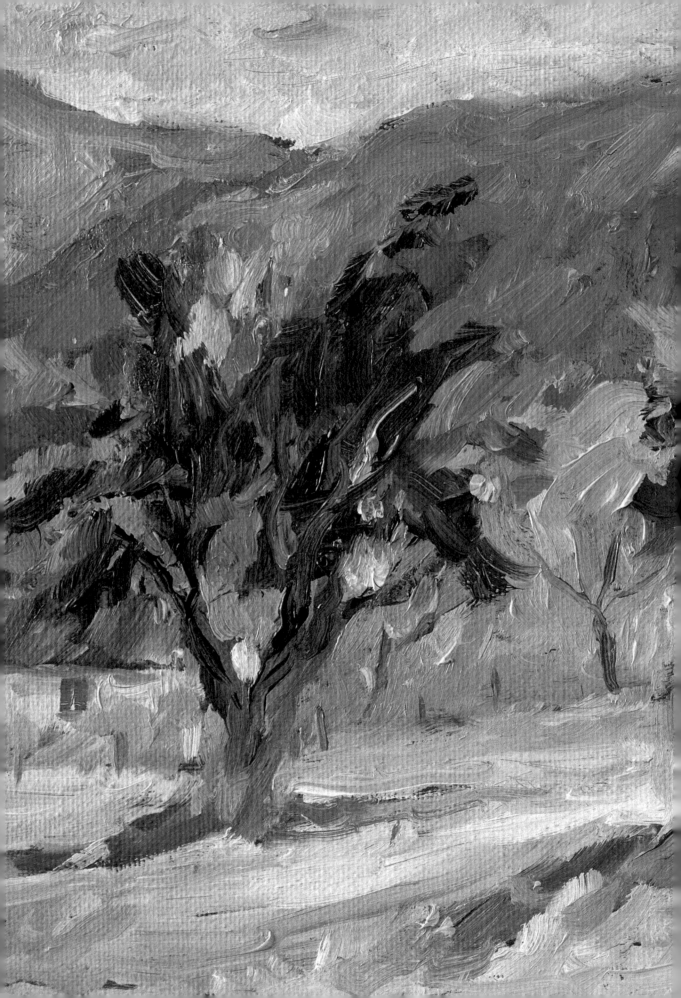

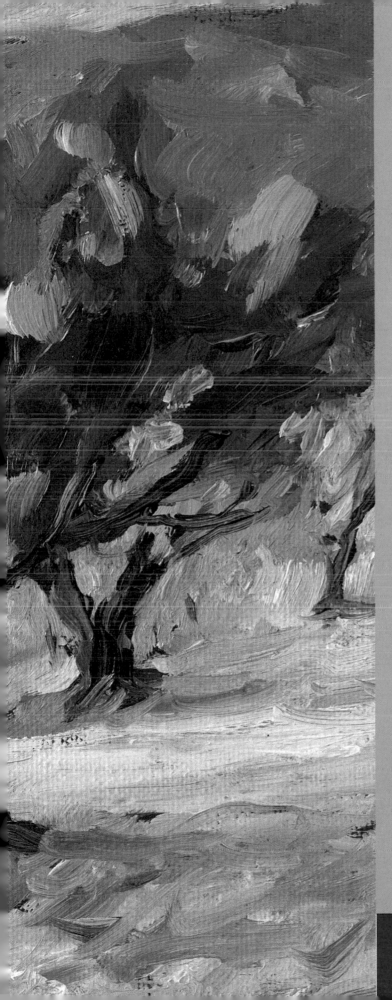

Getting Started

Now that you've decided
what equipment is essential,
it is now time to start
painting. But where to begin?
The first step is to know how
to use your oil paints by
discovering how many
different effects can be
created. This section will
guide you through basic
techniques as well as mixing
colors and coming to terms
with tones.

◀ The Olive Grove
20 x 25 cm (8 x 10 in)

GETTING TO KNOW OIL PAINT

In order to help you get a "feel" for oil paints, take a medium size sheet of sketching paper and simply play with the paint. Try to make as many different marks as possible. This may seem silly at first, but it is probably the best way to start because you will not be under any pressure to produce a painting, just a series of marks and experiments. Apply the paint thinly mixed with plenty of gel medium; try adding another color on top – use thicker paint; draw fine lines with the rigger brush; try to create "lively" brushstrokes, working a No. 4 flat brush in different directions every time you touch the canvas; even try scratching through an area of thicker paint.

You will see that there are infinite ways to create marks with oil paint. Also, oil paint can actually "feel" different depending on how it is used; for example, when thinned down with gel medium it is smooth and glossy, but used straight from the tube, it is much more "sticky" in texture.

BASIC TECHNIQUES

After you have tried some experiments with oil paint, try some of the following basic techniques. A technique is really a specific way of applying paint to canvas. The techniques shown here are some of the more common methods used. Practice them until you are confident in handling oil paint and achieving the effect you want.

▼ When you first start painting with oils, make as many marks as possible. Doodles like the ones below do not make any sense; they were simply fun to do.

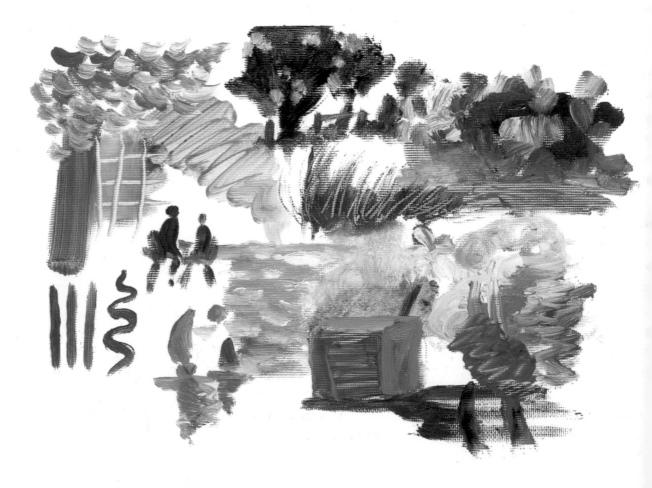

Scumbling

Scumbling is a useful way of creating an area of broken color. The paint is applied fairly thinly and using a "dry brush" (not dipped in thinner first of all) so that patches of the canvas or underlying color show through the scumbled top layer. This technique can be helpful in toning down an area of color that appears too strong or dark. A light blue shade can be scumbled over the top of the dry distant hillside to make it appear more distant in the painting

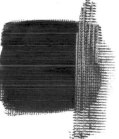

Blocking in

In order to establish the main areas at an early stage in the painting the larger shapes are "blocked in" with flat areas of solid color. Paint is applied with even brushstrokes, lightly mixed with thinner, to establish these opaque areas of color.

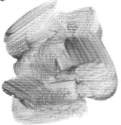

Stippling

Another technique for creating areas of broken color. Paint is dabbed onto the canvas, often on top of another dry color. Stippling can add texture and also break up a large flat area of color; for example, patches of red stippled onto a field of wheat can create the appearance of poppies in the middle distance.

Impasto

Paint is applied thickly using random brushstrokes to create a textured effect. Highlights in the sky and on the edges of buildings are areas where impasto is a useful tool. Heavily painted highlights stand out much better against the rest of the painting giving them much more emphasis than areas of dark tone.

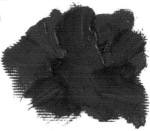

Brushstrokes

While not strictly a technique, the mark made by the brush in oil painting is a key element. For example, when painting a figure or animal a single brushstroke can be used for the arm or leg. Also, the brushstroke itself makes a textural mark in the paint, creating a more interesting surface than blended color. When painting skies, these brushstrokes can be used in a pattern to help create the cloud shapes and give a sense of movement.

Random lines

Use random lines to add branches and other linear details over wet paint. Dragging a rigger brush through the wet underpainting picks up a little of the underlying color, blending in and creating a very natural effect.

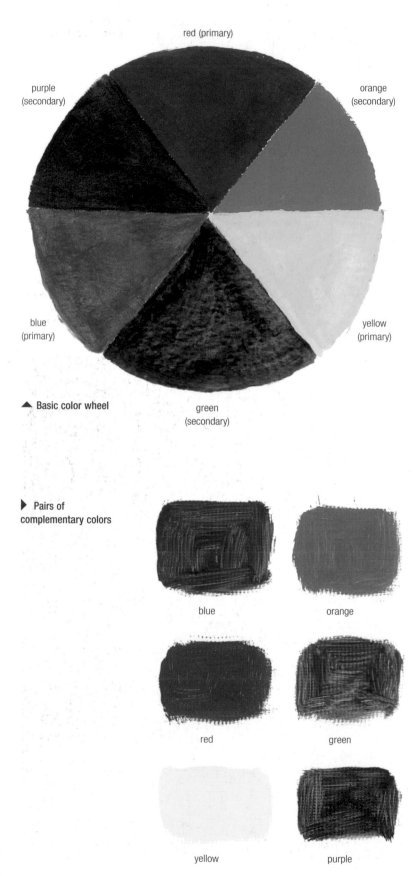

red (primary)

orange
(secondary)

purple
(secondary)

blue
(primary)

yellow
(primary)

green
(secondary)

▲ Basic color wheel

▶ Pairs of
complementary colors

blue

orange

red

green

yellow

purple

MIXING COLORS

Color theory sounds a dry subject, so it is
tempting to skip over this section.
Learning how colors work is important
in painting, however. By following these
simple guidelines, I hope you will find
mixing colors interesting and easy to
understand.

Most students remember the basic
color wheel that shows the three primary
and secondary colors.

Colors that are opposite each other on
the wheel are termed complementary.
Therefore, blue and orange are
complementary to each other, as are
yellow and purple, and red and green.
Colors that are complementary will
make gray when they are mixed together
in equal portions. If you add a little
orange into blue it will "gray down" the
blue, making it slightly darker, softer
and duller. This is a very useful
technique for landscape painting. That is
all you really need to remember about
color theory. The secret lies in
understanding how to use this
knowledge when mixing colors.

Darker shades and shadow colors

We can use this knowledge of
complementary colors to make darker
shades and shadow tones rather than
simply adding black. Only a very small
amount of a color's complementary will
considerably darken it in tone. For
example, a touch of viridian added to
alizarin crimson will produce a dark or
dull red. Similarly, a touch of alizarin
crimson added to viridian will darken or
dull the green. Try this for yourself and

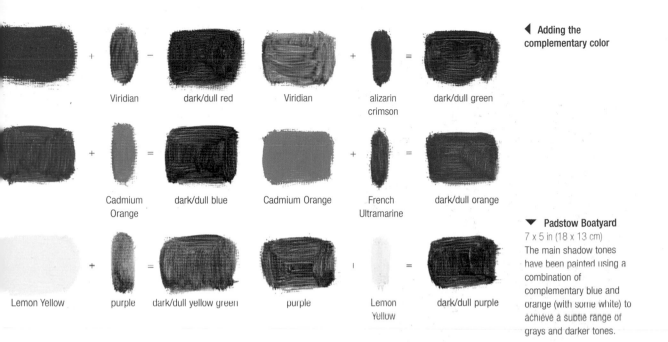

	+ Viridian	− dark/dull red	Viridian	+ alizarin crimson	= dark/dull green		
	+ Cadmium Orange	= dark/dull blue	Cadmium Orange	+ French Ultramarine	= dark/dull orange		
Lemon Yellow	+ purple	= dark/dull yellow green	purple		Lemon Yellow	= dark/dull purple	

◀ **Adding the complementary color**

▼ **Padstow Boatyard**
7 x 5 in (18 x 13 cm)
The main shadow tones have been painted using a combination of complementary blue and orange (with some white) to achieve a subtle range of grays and darker tones.

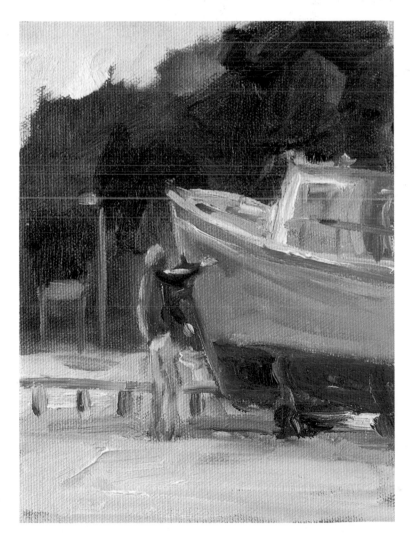

hen with other complementary pairs of olors. Being able to darken a color in his way without making it appear dirty elps to keep the whole painting alive ith clean colors, avoiding the tendency o create "mud."

Putting theory into practice

s you start to mix darker shades with more confidence you will tend to use hem more. For example, when painting ees, use your chosen green for the ghter side of the tree and indicate the hadow side by darkening the green with little red. When painting figures, using darker shade on one side can help give rm; for instance, a little blue purple dded to the mix for a yellow jacket and sed on one side would give some shape the figure. Similarly, boats which are ometimes brightly painted still need a hadow side; a little orange mixed into a right blue for the hull darkens it to give hape to the bottom of the boat.

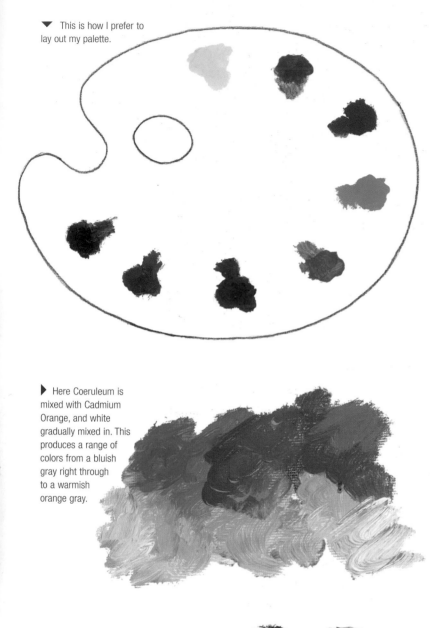

▼ This is how I prefer to lay out my palette.

▶ Here Coeruleum is mixed with Cadmium Orange, and white gradually mixed in. This produces a range of colors from a bluish gray right through to a warmish orange gray.

▶ This time French Ultramarine is mixed with Cadmium Orange. Can you see the fairly subtle difference in gray tones from the Coeruleum mix?

MIXING COLORFUL GRAYS

When painting landscapes, grays and soft blues are constantly required, not only for skies but also to indicate background hills and create a feeling of space and distance. By using only four colors, two blues and two orange shades, with the addition of some white, you will be able to mix a whole range of subtle gray tones. I am always mixing gray tones and find it most helpful to place the key colors that I use alongside each other on my palette.

Start off by placing your colors in the same order on the palette as shown here with the two blues and two orange shades next to each other in the center of the palette. This will create a "key mixing zone," essentially a simple reminder for mixing gray tones, so important for landscape painting.

Try mixing a series of grays for yourself. Start off using only cadmium orange, first with cerulean blue, then with French ultramarine. This brighter orange color makes a "clean" gray when mixed with blue. Then repeat the exercise using light red in place of cadmium orange. The grays will be much stronger but may appear a little muddy, particularly if you add too much light red. Adding white to your mixtures will considerably increase the range of grays.

COPING WITH GREENS

Green is everywhere in the landscape and, as an artist, it is very easy to be overwhelmed by it. As with all colors, however, green is usually tinged with another color; for instance, it may be a

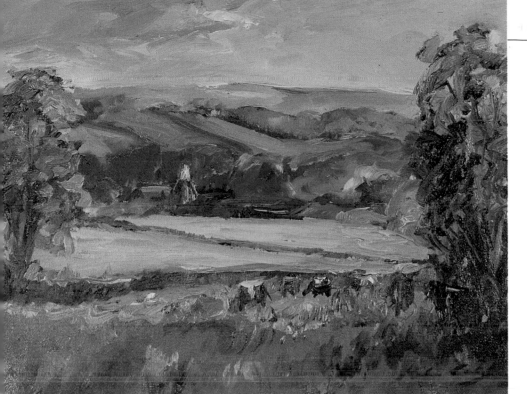

◀ **Across the Kentish Weald**
28 x 36 cm (11 x 14 in)
In this view over the Kentish Weald on a wet, gray day when all the greens looked much the same, differences have been exaggerated to create a feeling of recession, using stronger tones in the foreground and much bluer shades towards the distant hills.

eddish green shade or a bright lime green or even have a warm ocher undertone. So, when you start to mix greens, be aware of the differences within the color rather than regarding every tree, field, or bush as simply "green." Ask yourself what sort of green it is, and you will see these differences. When painting, exaggerate the variations to keep the whole painting alive and to avoid a flat look that happens when you use only one or two shades of green.

Using Viridian

In principle, mixing blue and yellow makes green. Mixing cerulean and lemon yellow produces a range of bright greens, but not all blues and yellows make good green shades. So, I suggest you try mixing greens using viridian as a base color. On its own, viridian looks strong and unnatural, but when mixed with either of the two yellows, or orange, or even its complementary, red, a whole range of natural tones can be created.

exercise

Look carefully at the greens in the landscape – how many different shades can you really see? Make quick sketches and note down the tones on different areas of the sketch; for instance, whether one tree is reddish in tone or more ocher colored.

Lemon Yellow added   Raw Sienna added

Viridian

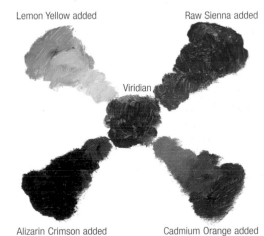

Alizarin Crimson added   Cadmium Orange added

◀ **Using viridian as a base green**

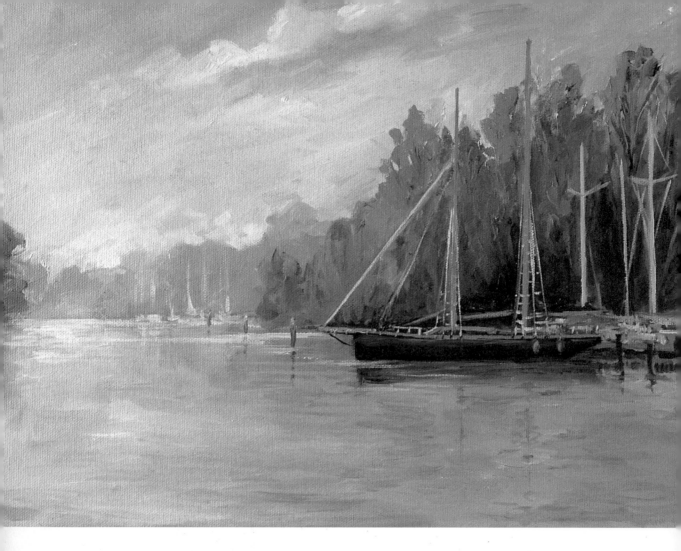

▲ **Quiet Moorings, River Hamble**
12 x 16 in (31 x 41 cm)
On a misty morning it is easier to judge tones than on a bright sunny day because the atmosphere intervenes and simplifies matters. Distant trees appear as simple shapes, and even foreground features lose some detail, making it easier to judge their relative tonal value.

▼ A simple tonal scale from black to white

WHAT IS TONE?

Every color has a range of tones from its brightest version to its darkest, and the tonal value of a color is simply its relative lightness or darkness. The term tonal values within a painting refers to the overall range of lights to darks in the composition. Before you start a painting, it is essential to sort out what is the lightest area and how light is it? Similarly what is the darkest area and how dark is it? Every other color in the painting will fall somewhere in between these two extremes of light and dark.

To help you assess the tone of a color, make a simple tonal scale using black and white paint. Start with pure black and gradually add white until you reach pure white. Try to have at least six different stages in between. Keep this scale beside you as a reminder while you are painting.

Tonal sketches

Tonal sketches are a simple way to begin to understand tones. Making a tonal sketch is, in effect, painting in monochrome. One way in which to practice how to recognize and achieve these variations in tone is to make sketches from photographs. You will need to look carefully at your photographs to decide not only which areas are dark and which light, but also how light or how dark they are. In the two examples I have painted here I have used French ultramarine and a little raw sienna for the warmer light tones, but the overall effect is the same as if I had used only one color.

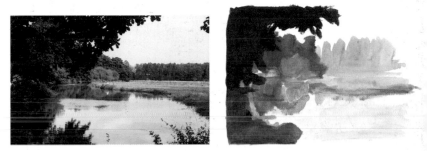

▲ The photograph of Kefallonia appears fairly flat, but notice that the background mountain is, in fact, slightly darker than the one in front of it. The sky and water are almost the same tone, while the lighter side of the foreground house is the lightest part of the whole picture.

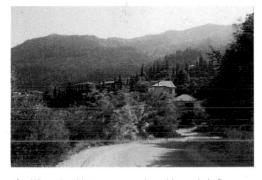

▲ A tonal sketch is particularly useful for a subject containing many different greens. In this photograph the furthest trees are palest in tone, while the foreground branches are the darkest.

exercise

Use these photographs to create your own tonal sketches. Keep to a small scale, say 10 x 15 cm (4 x 6 in) maximum, and try to work fairly quickly, giving yourself about 15 minutes for each one. Then try some quick tonal sketches of your own photographs.

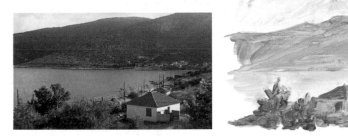

▲ When sketching a scene, such as this one in Lefkas, Greece, be sure there is a difference in tonal value between the middle-ground aand the distance (fir trees and the hill, in this case).

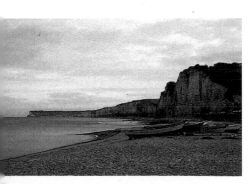

This photograph of the cliffs near Etretat in France was taken on a particularly dull day. The camera shows the cliff as one tone. To create a sense of distance, however, the further cliffs should appear much lighter in tone.

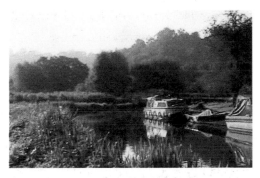

▲ A misty morning on the River Wey shows fairly clearly the tonal contrasts from the distant trees to the foreground riverbank.

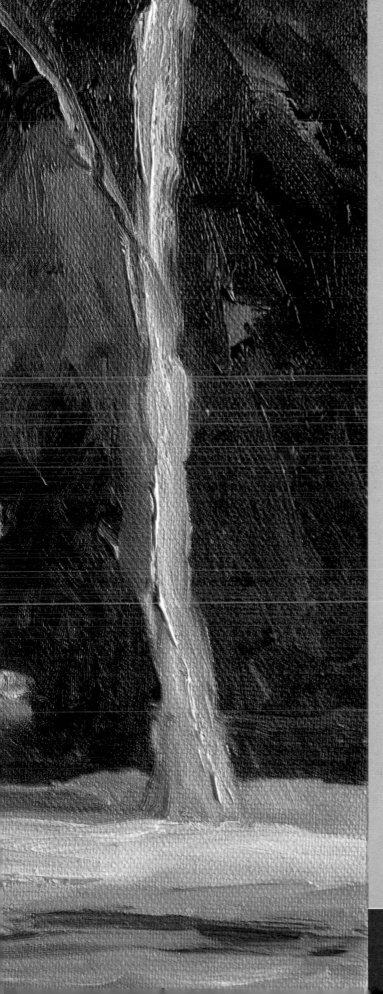

Simplifying Composition

Composition and perspective are probably two of the most unpopular aspects of painting! Having to deal with them can strike fear in the beginner, and even more experienced artists can become confused when trying to understand the finer points of linear perspective. Since this is a book about landscape painting, I have tried to suggest basic guidelines for you to follow rather than presenting too much detail and theory.

◀ **Loire Château**
10 x 12 in (25 x 31 cm)

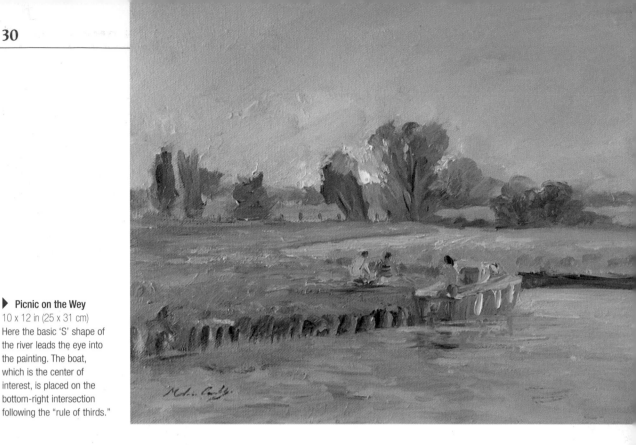

▶ **Picnic on the Wey**
10 x 12 in (25 x 31 cm)
Here the basic 'S' shape of
the river leads the eye into
the painting. The boat,
which is the center of
interest, is placed on the
bottom-right intersection
following the "rule of thirds."

SIMPLE GUIDELINES

Composition is simply the arrangement
of shapes within a painting in order to
create an appealing and well-balanced
picture. These main shapes are often
used to guide the eye of the viewer to
one point in the picture – the focal point
or main point of interest. This sounds
fairly easy, and it should be, provided
you are aware of some basic guidelines.
First of all, try to avoid placing the

horizon line exactly halfway up the
canvas. This will divide the painting in
two and immediately set off a conflict in
the composition. Any other division of
the canvas should avoid this problem.
Secondly, try not to place the main point
of interest in the absolute center of the
picture. A central point of interest makes
for a very dull composition.

Rule of thirds

Another useful guideline is the "rule of
thirds." Divide up the canvas into
sections, using both horizontal and
vertical lines. Placing the main point of
interest at one of the four junction
points on the canvas helps create a
balanced structure to the painting.
Similarly, placing the horizon on one of
the two horizontal lines – that is, either
one third from the top or bottom of the
canvas – will also form the basis for a
good composition.

Point of interest at one of
the four junction points.

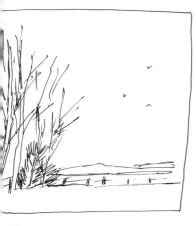

▲ 'L'-shape
strong vertical on one side of the picture, with a
ong horizontal foreground. The main point of
erest usually occurs within the angle.

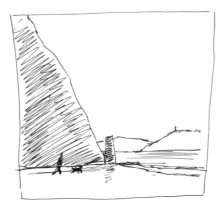

▲ Diagonal
A diagonal line running across the canvas can
look very effective. However, make sure it creates
an interesting shape and divides the canvas into
two uneven parts.

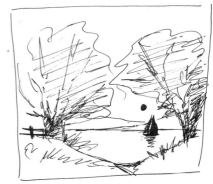

▲ Tunnel
A tunnel or 'O' shape is often found in nature
where trees overhang. Similar shapes can be seen
in townscapes; for instance, through an archway
or window. Take care to place both the 'O' shape
and main interest off center to avoid symmetry.

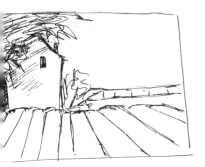

▲ Radiating lines
ne of fencing, buildings or even rows of
ender can be used to guide the eye towards the
in point of interest.

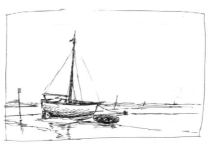

▲ Group
With a group of figures, boats or even trees as the
main subject, the group can be placed off center,
perhaps along one of the lines dividing the canvas
following the 'rule of thirds'.

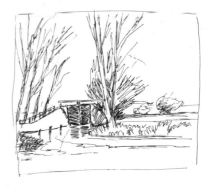

▲ 'S'-shape
A road or river can be used to lead the eye
through the painting to the main point of interest.

asic compositional shapes

ny number of different compositional
apes can be used to lead the eye to a
cal point to make an interesting
cture. A few compositional shapes are
own above to get you started.

sing a viewfinder

nding potential compositional shapes
the landscape is not always obvious. A
mple viewfinder will help you plan
ur compositions. Cut two L-shaped
eces of cardboard and hold them
gether to make a frame; move them to
atch the proportions of your canvas.

Start by holding the viewfinder at
arm's length in front of your subject –
for example, the local church. The
viewfinder cuts out much of the
surrounding scene, enabling you to
concentrate on the church itself. As you
bring the viewfinder nearer to your eye,
the scene within it increases, taking in
more of the neighboring countryside.
Once you have decided on your view,
note any features on the edge and paint
from, say, the tree on the left to the bush
on the right. These key marker points
will mean you do not need to constantly
refer to the viewfinder.

POTENTIAL PITFALLS

It can be very tempting to include every feature in front of you, even when it detracts from the overall effect. If there is an ugly water tower on the left, for example, leave it out. Similarly with trees and other natural objects – it can be much better to keep just the main forms and leave out those that do not add anything to the overall composition.

GETTING EVERYTHING IN PERSPECTIVE

For the purposes of landscape painting, the key starting point for correct perspective is the horizon line or eye level. To find eye level, hold your arm full stretch in front of you with your thumb pointing upward. Look past the top of your thumb into the distance – you are looking at eye level. The term "vanishing point" is used to describe the place on the eye line where two parallel lines (such as tramlines) appear to converge in the far distance.

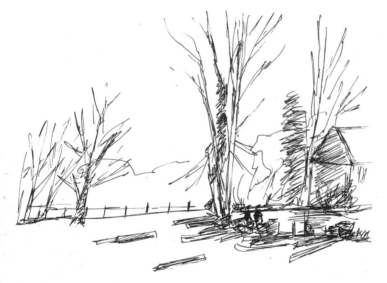

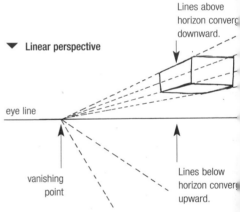

▼ **Linear perspective**

Lines above horizon converge downward.

eye line

vanishing point

Lines below horizon converge upward.

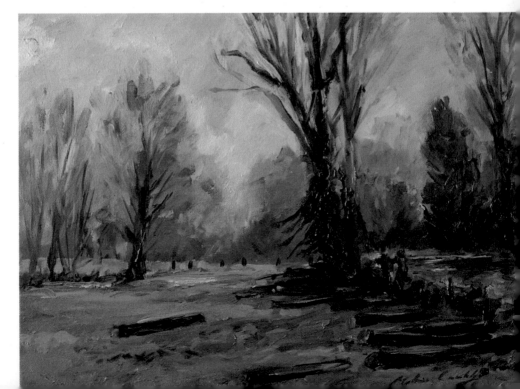

▲ ▶ **Tree Felling, Ripley**
10 x 12 in (25 x 31 cm)
In this view of tree felling near the River Wey I decided to leave out the farmhouse on the far right since this was at the very edge of the view and would have led the eye out of the painting rather than keeping it within the L-shape framework of the composition.

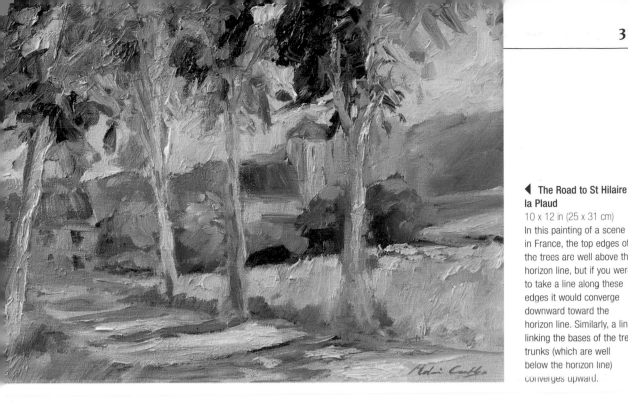

When you draw the horizon onto your canvas it stands in place of the eye line. Above this horizon horizontal lines converge downward to the vanishing point, but horizontal lines below the horizon will appear to rise up to the vanishing point.

AERIAL PERSPECTIVE

Just as important to the artist is the way in which the intervening atmosphere affects the colors you see in the landscape. The further away you are from a subject, the more atmosphere there will be between you and the subject, hence the greater the effect of the atmosphere on the colors before you. This is known as aerial perspective. Colors recede in strength toward the horizon, becoming not only paler but considerably bluer. Detail is also much less – you cannot see individual branches when you are several miles away!

This effect of intervening atmosphere is most obvious on a misty or foggy day.

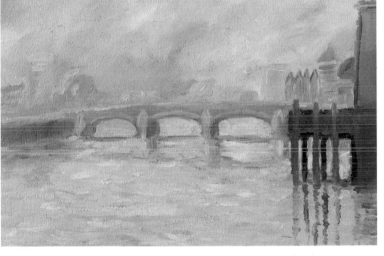

▲ Chelsea Reach
5 x 7 in (13 x 18 cm)
In misty conditions even complex subjects are reduced to a series of simple shapes.

Distant trees or hills may disappear completely into the mist, and even middle distance trees appear much paler and with far less color than on a clear day. The key point to remember here is that the atmosphere still has a subtle effect even on a sunny day, and it is essential as an artist that you are both aware of this and exaggerate its effect in your paintings.

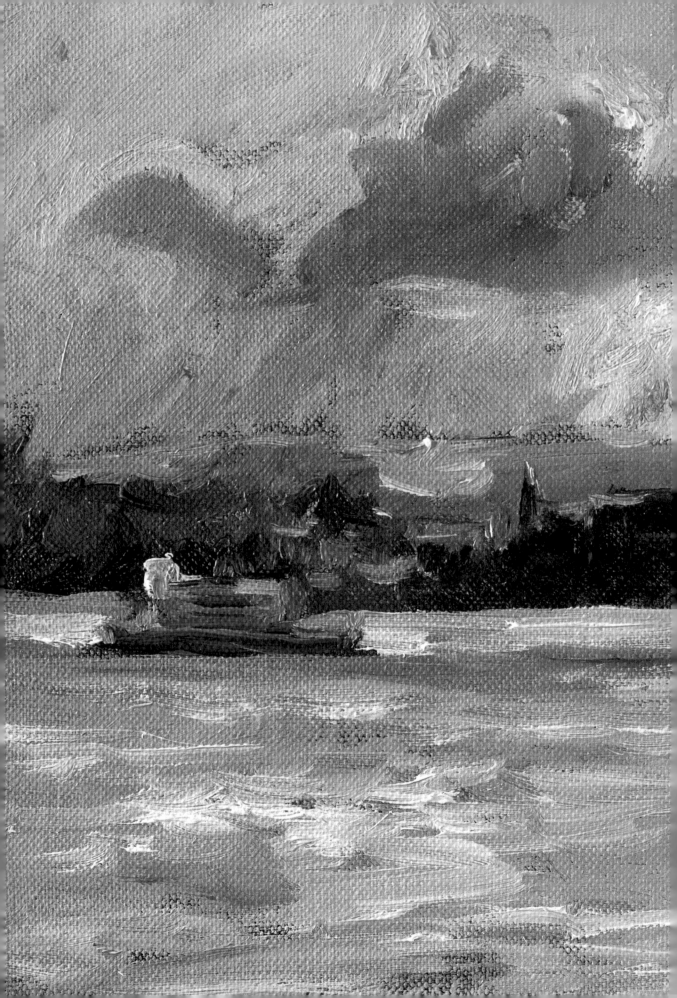

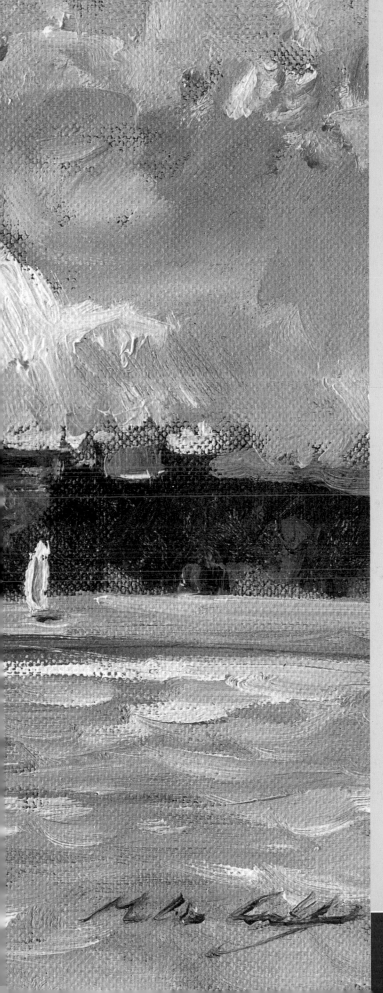

Sky and Clouds

The sky dictates the mood of a painting, and all the other elements in the scene reflect this mood. Oil paint is an excellent medium for conveying the sky: the soft edges of clouds can be created with a brush or the fingers, and the highlights on the defined top edges of larger clouds can be emphasized by applying paint thickly with a knife.

◀ Passing Shower, Isle of Wight
20 x 25 cm (8 x 10 in)

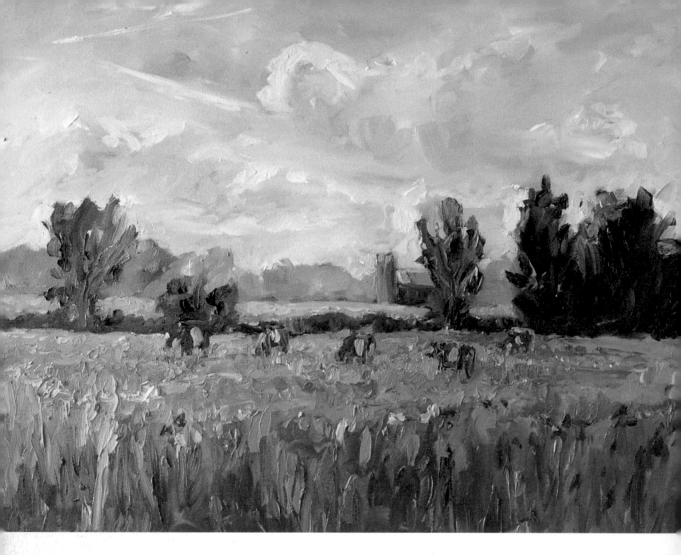

▲ **Watermeadows, Send Marsh**

16 x 20 in (41 x 51 cm)
For this painting I tinted the canvas with burnt sienna to give it a warm orange tone. Small patches of the underpainting can be seen in both the meadow and sky. The effect under the pale blue colors of the sky is particularly successful.

USING A COLORED GROUND

Now it is time to actually start painting. The first consideration is whether to work on a white or colored background. I rarely paint onto a white background because this makes it much more difficult to judge the lightest tones – white paint does not show up on white canvas. Having a medium-toned surface instead enables you to judge the lightest and darkest tones immediately.

Part of the joy of oil painting is the range of textures possible, and even leaving a little of the underlying canvas showing through can be very effective. If the canvas surface is white, it rarely adds anything to the finished painting.

However, if you start with a thin wash of burnt sienna or a mix of cerulean blue and cadmium orange, allowing this wash to dry thoroughly first, then the warm tone has a subtle effect on the finished painting, particularly on the sky.

In watercolor the usual procedure is to first paint the sky, using large washes. But beginning with the sky is not always possible in painting with oils. You will need to decide whether to paint the sky first, leaving space for any trees or buildings, or to paint the sky last and work up to the background shapes. Unless the sky is the predominant area of the painting, where the horizon line is very low, for example, then I would recommend painting the sky last.

LIGHT SOURCE

It's easy to make the mistake in painting of having more than one light source. I often draw an arrow as I'm sketching indicating the direction of light. On the actual painting, mark in all the shadow areas in blue and the highlights with a little white at the same time when you draw in the composition. This guarantees that all the shadows show light coming from the same direction.

tip

• *There is proportion within the sky as in the landscape. Clouds nearer to the viewer appear larger, but also higher. Toward the horizon clouds appear smaller and colors weaker.*

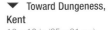

▼ **Toward Dungeness, Kent**
10 x 12 in (25 x 31 cm)
This coastal view was painted during the afternoon looking directly into the light. Because the clouds were lit from within, they were created using yellow ocher and cerulean blue, with a light edge outlining them.

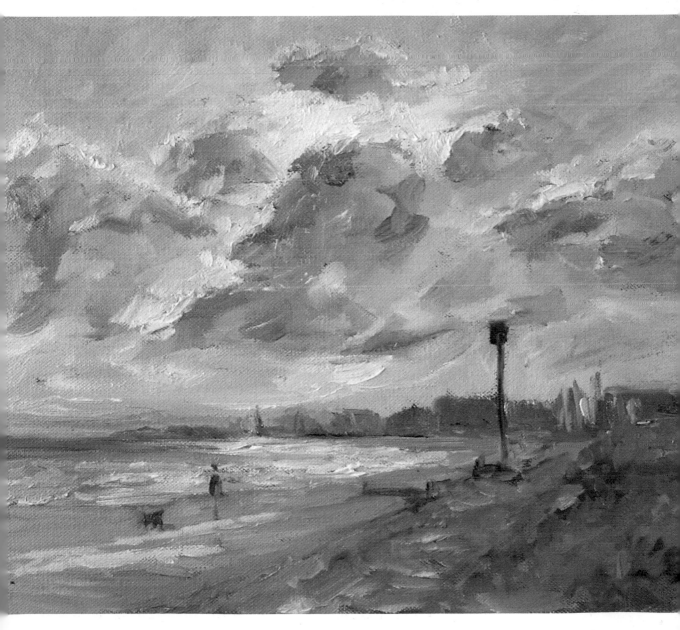

▶ Clear sky

UNDERSTANDING CLOUDS

In order to learn to paint various cloud types, start by copying the examples shown here. Use oil sketching paper and allow 15 minutes for each one. Work to a small scale – no larger, say, than 4 x 6 in (10 x 15 cm) – but use a ⅝ in (16 mm) flat brush. Try not to add too much gel medium and clean your brush only at the end of each exercise. If you find the colors are getting muddy, wipe off any excess paint with a rag or paper towels.

▼ Summer cumulus

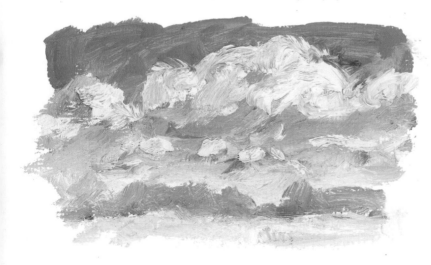

Clear sky

Start at the top using a mixture of cerulean blue, French ultramarine, and white. Gradually work toward the horizon, changing the mixture to cerulea and white only, and then using a little yellow ocher and white just above the horizon to create a haze effect. Now add very simple clouds using alizarin crimso and French ultramarine. Finally, indicate distant hills with French ultramarine, alizarin crimson, and white to give a sens of scale.

Summer cumulus

Cumulus clouds are the fluffy ones we se on a summer day. Start at the top of the paper with the strongest blue tone – agai a mix of cerulean and French ultramarin Place a few patches of blue, then wipe your brush and pick up some white pain tinged with a little lemon yellow and cadmium orange. Use this to indicate the tops of the clouds. Add yellow ocher and

ouch of cerulean blue for the undersides.
eneath the clouds, blue tones in the sky
re much softer. Use cerulean blue and
hite with a little cadmium orange to
ray the color.

Mackerel sky with vapor trails

hese thin high cloud patterns appear
omplicated, but they are actually easy to
aint. Start as if painting a clear sky using
erulean blue and French ultramarine,
lended downward and changing the
ixture to cerulean blue and white only.
hen load the brush with white and
ellow ocher (for a soft cream) and dab on
mall patches of color, adding a few dabs
 the cerulean blue and white mixture in
laces. A single swift brushstroke creates
e vapor trail. Indicate the horizon line
ith yellow ocher and viridian.

Storm clouds

sing a mixture of French ultramarine,
admium orange, and white, mix a
lection of gray tones. Starting with the
alest gray, scrub in the overall cloud
ea, leaving a small section near the top
r the light to break through. Paint over
is cloud with the other gray tones,
eping your paint fairly "dry" (with very
tle gel medium), to create shapes within
is clouded area. Wipe excess paint from
e brush and mix a little cadmium
range into white for the patch of
nlight. Having indicated a horizon with
ridian and raw sienna, use short
ownward brushstrokes for sunlight
tering below the cloud. Paint directly
to the wet green tone of the horizon,
otting out the horizon here and there.

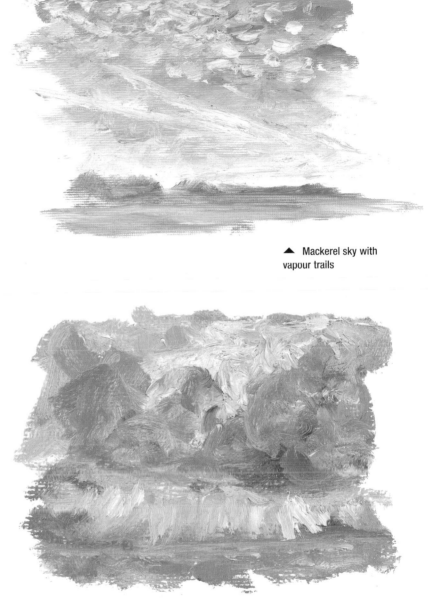

▲ Mackerel sky with
vapour trails

▲ Storm clouds

tip

◆ Use a ⅝ in (16 mm) flat brush for all of
these exercises and apply the paint quickly
using fast "scrubby" marks to give vitality to
your work.

CHANGING LIGHT

Attempting to catch the changing light in the sky from morning to evening appears rather daunting at first. Not only does the sky vary tremendously with the changing pattern of clouds overhead, but also, the overall color and light in the sky will change during the day, from predominantly yellow in the morning, more blue toward midday, and then to warmish pink/orange undertones in the evening. This is a generalization of the color changes; the seasons will add their own subtle variations. In winter, particularly, skies are often more colorful because the strength of the sun is reduced, while summer skies appear bleached, almost white, on clear middays, offering little inspiration to the outdoor painter.

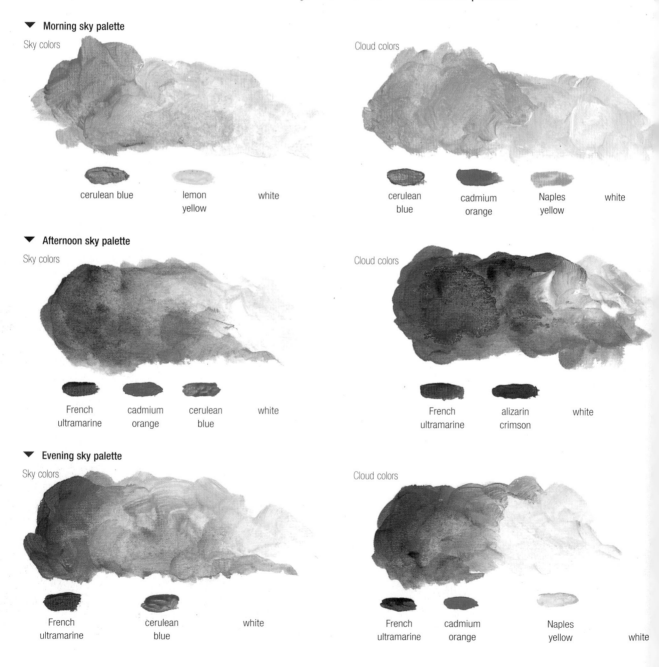

▼ **Morning sky palette**

Sky colors

| cerulean blue | lemon yellow | white |

Cloud colors

| cerulean blue | cadmium orange | Naples yellow | white |

▼ **Afternoon sky palette**

Sky colors

| French ultramarine | cadmium orange | cerulean blue | white |

Cloud colors

| French ultramarine | alizarin crimson | white |

▼ **Evening sky palette**

Sky colors

| French ultramarine | cerulean blue | white |

Cloud colors

| French ultramarine | cadmium orange | Naples yellow | white |

Morning sky

The morning sky often has a yellowish tinge; you see this especially along the horizon. In settled conditions clouds tend to be wispy and strung out. Dawn mists also add to the hazy effect of the morning sky. If you wish to create the effect of mist, use a glaze of French ultramarine and cadmium orange applied very thinly over the painting to build up a misty layer along the base of the trees or just above the water on a river scene. This is a very subtle technique and you may need to apply several layers to achieve the desired effect.

The morning palette consists of a blend of turquoise blues and warm yellow tones and might include cerulean blue, French ultramarine, cadmium orange, yellow ocher, Naples yellow, and titanium white.

▼ **Morning Light, Shoreham**
12 x 16 in (31 x 41 cm)
This painting was produced on location on a bright winter morning. Some clouds have started to billow up but are fairly thin and spread out. The rising sun is behind them, and its rays shine through onto the cottage roofs. Sunlight tones are a blend of cadmium orange, yellow ocher, and plenty of white to give a very pale gold.

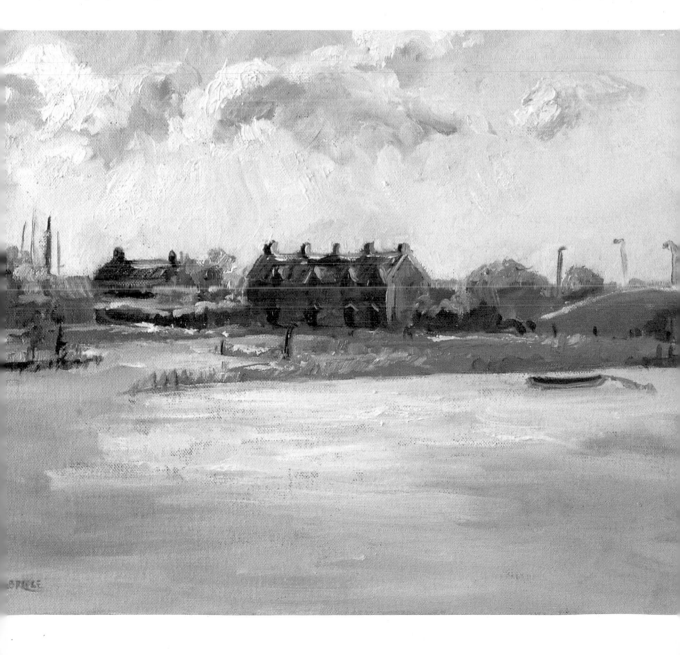

Afternoon sky

Clouds are usually much more in evidence during the afternoon. These summer clouds are easy to paint provided you use the brushstrokes to create a sense of movement, as I have done in *View from Titsey Hill*. In summer the heat of the day will cause cumulus clouds to build up. In winter more turbulent weather conditions bring storm clouds, rain, and very dramatic skies. These winter skies can appear very dark, indeed, but be careful not to mix your colors too strongly otherwise they will overpower the landscape underneat and may appear rather unrealistic. A mixture of French ultramarine and alizarin crimson makes a good basic purple, but this will need to be "grayed down" using a little cadmium orange to take away its intensity. Adding white wil enable you to reach the desired shade.

The afternoon palette consists of French ultramarine, cerulean blue, alizarin crimson, cadmium orange, and titanium white.

▼ **View from Titsey Hill**
10 x 12 in (25 x 31 cm)
As I painted this view while sitting on top of Titsey Hill looking out toward London, cumulus clouds were piling up. I painted them fairly rapidly using a mixture of French ultramarine, alizarin crimson, and white. Highlights were done with white and cadmium orange, and the surrounding blue with mainly cerulean.

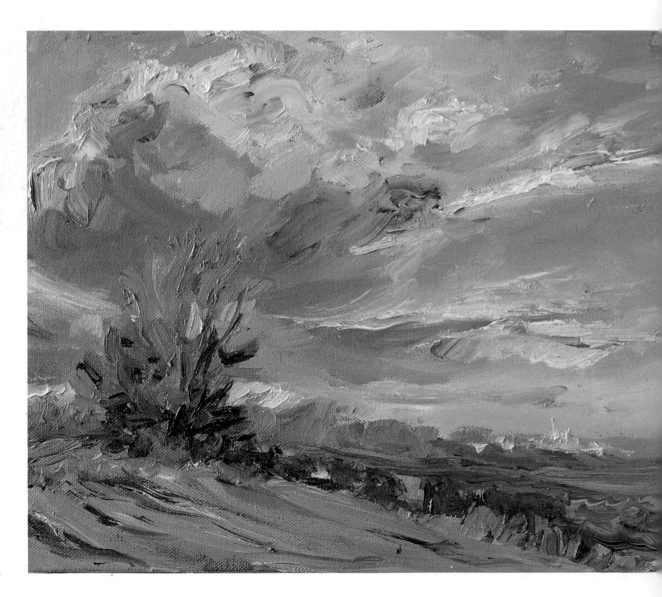

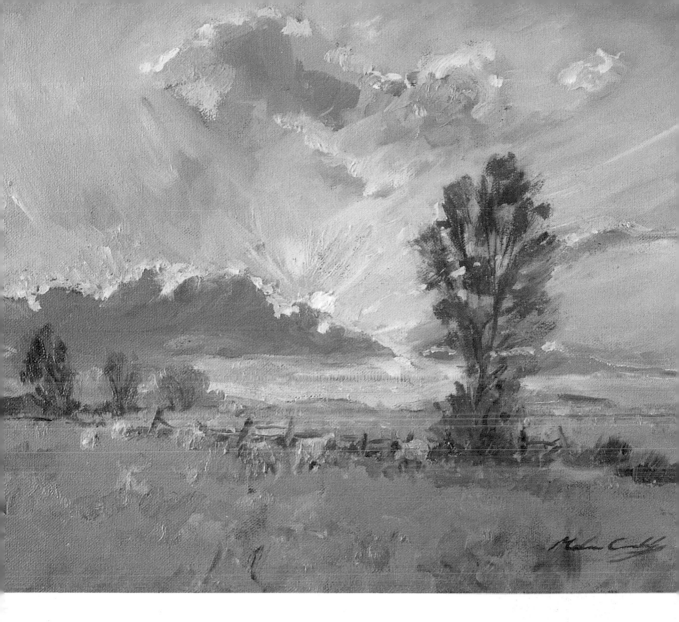

vening sky

s evening approaches and the sun sinks
w toward the horizon, its rays catch the
ouds and turn some of them to gold
gainst the darkening turquoise sky.
unsets are very exciting to paint, with
n almost unlimited range of colors. It is
asy to overdo them, however, by
ainting them too bright and cheerful.
avoid falling into this trap, place the
rongest yellow and orange tones only at
e center of the sunset, or on the sun
self if this is part of the painting, or in
e highlights on the clouds caught in
e sun's rays. Toward the top of the sky,

colors are usually much softer and the
blues often quite dark. A little alizarin
crimson added to these blues will darken
them and give some purple warmth to
the top of the sky. Sunsets vary so much
that simply sitting watching the sun as it
sets can be the best way to improve your
sunset paintings. It is helpful to make
quick sketches in pencil, making lots of
color notes to remind you of each one.

The evening palette includes cerulean
blue, French ultramarine, cadmium
orange, raw sienna, lemon yellow,
cadmium yellow deep, alizarin crimson,
and titanium white.

▲ **Sunset over Romney
Marsh**
11 x 14 in (28 x 36 cm)
This sunset was painted on
location, which meant
working extremely quickly.
I indicated the main clouds,
using cadmium orange and
cerulean blue for the darker
ones, with raw sienna and
cerulean blue for the upper,
sunlit cloud. Sunlit edges
were added using lemon
yellow, cadmium orange,
and white and blended
upward into the sky to
create the effect of the
sun's rays.

demonstration
Norfolk Sky

The wide open landscapes of Norfolk, England, are ideal locations for painting skies. Since clouds change rapidly, however, particularly on breezy days, it is probably easier to work from photographs and sketches. Make plenty of rapid pencil sketches of clouds to develop a sense of movement, and mark in the position of the sun to work out which edges of the clouds will have highlights and shadows.

you will need

canvas 10 x 12 in (25 x 30 cm) (primed with acrylic burnt sienna)
brushes: No. 8 short flat, No. 4 short flat, No. 4 round, No. 10 short flat

colors

French ultramarine, light red, cadmium orange, lemon yellow, raw sienna, cerulean blue, viridian, sap green, alizarin crimson, and titanium white.

tips

• *Painting a blue horizon creates a sense of distance in the picture.*

• *Make the initial shadow area of the cloud a little larger than it will be in the finished painting.*

• *Keep your brush clean by wiping off excess paint rather than using turpentine. This will prevent the brush from becoming too wet. A dryish brush is essential to make the most of the brushmarks.*

• *Paint the highlights on the clouds much thicker than the shadow side. This makes them much more effective.*

• *Try to finish the sky in about half an hour. Working quickly keeps the brushstrokes lively and helps you maintain concentration.*

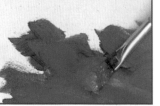

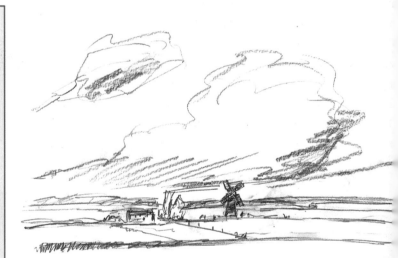

▲ **STEP ONE**

The initial sketch concentrated on the overa shape of the main cloud. I drew it rapidly with sweeping lines to give an impression o movement. The horizon is low down in the composition, leaving plenty of space for the clouds. The buildings and windmill act as a focal point.

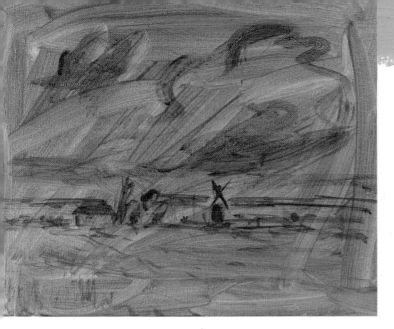

◀ STEP TWO

I primed the canvas with a wash of burnt sienna, using acrylic rather than oil paint since it dries quickly and allows me to start painting almost immediately. Painting on a warm undertone is particularly helpful for sky subjects. Using a No. 4 flat brush and French ultramarine, I marked in the horizon, foreground buildings, and the two main cloud shapes, including their shadow sides.

▶ STEP THREE

The horizon line was painted using French ultramarine and white, with a little viridian and raw sienna added to the mixture as I painted down toward the line of buildings. The left-hand building was painted with raw sienna and French ultramarine, and I used light red and French ultramarine to establish the darker shape of the windmill. Both these shapes were painted with a No. 4 round brush. The trees alongside are sap green and raw sienna.

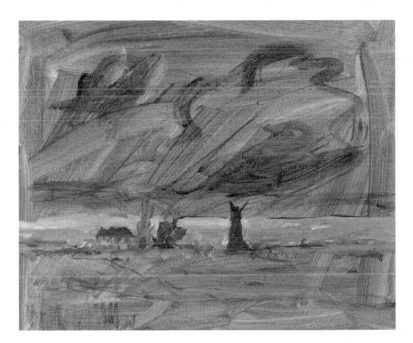

◀ STEP FOUR

With the horizon and middle ground established, I could turn my attention to the sky. The whole sky is painted with No. 10 flat brush. This might seem too large a brush for such a small canvas, but the key to painting large clouds successfully is to use the individual brushmarks to create an impression of movement. I started at the top of the canvas with a mix of French ultramarine, cerulean blue, and just a little white, and painted the blue sky down to the top edge of the clouds.

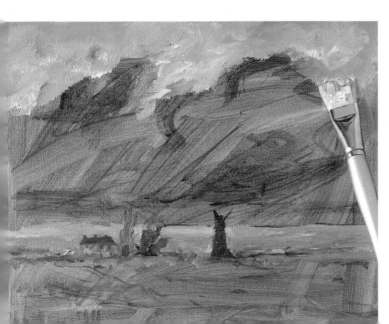

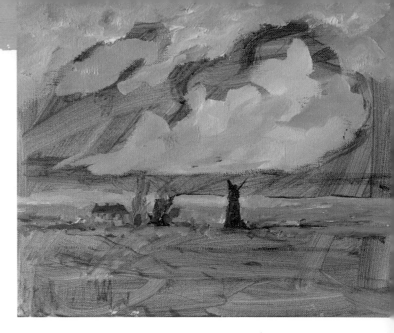

▶ **STEP FIVE**

I mixed alizarin crimson, French ultramarine, and white for a soft gray tone and blocked in the cloud from its bottom edge. This would form the shadow base to the clouds and give some color to blend into when the top half of the cloud is added.

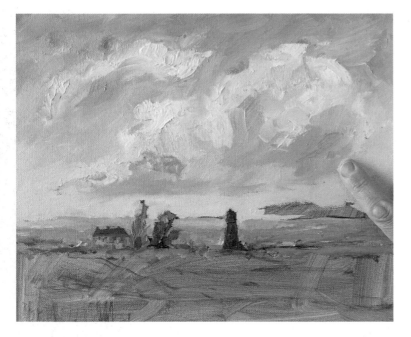

◀ **STEP SIX**

After wiping off the paint from my brush, I loaded it with color for the top of the cloud (using mainly white with a little cadmium orange to start). I applied the paint thickly and with definite brushstrokes, working in different directions to create cloud shapes. Then I blended this lighter color over some of the shadow tone, adding a very little raw sienna to the center of the cloud. I painted around the clouds using cerulean blue and white, making the color paler and adding a little cadmium orange where the sky meets the horizon. I blended the bottom edge of the cloud with my fingers for a softer effect.

▶ **STEP SEVEN**

With the sky completed, I used a No. 8 flat brush to scrub in the foreground with sap green and raw sienna. Darker areas were produced by adding cadmium orange to the sap green, and the hedgerow was also marked in using this mixture.

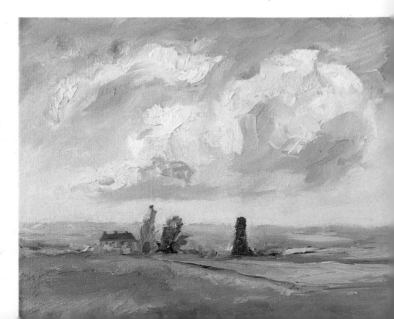

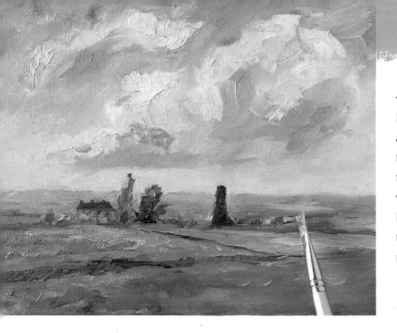

◀ **STEP EIGHT**

I painted more detail and used the sap green and cadmium orange mixture as a dark tone for the extra bushes and ditch across the foreground. Texture was given to this area with lemon yellow and cadmium orange. Finally (*see below*), I used a No. 4 round brush to paint sails on the windmill and to add a row of fence posts along the central hedgerow.

▼ **Norfolk Sky** 10 x 12 in (25 x 30 cm)

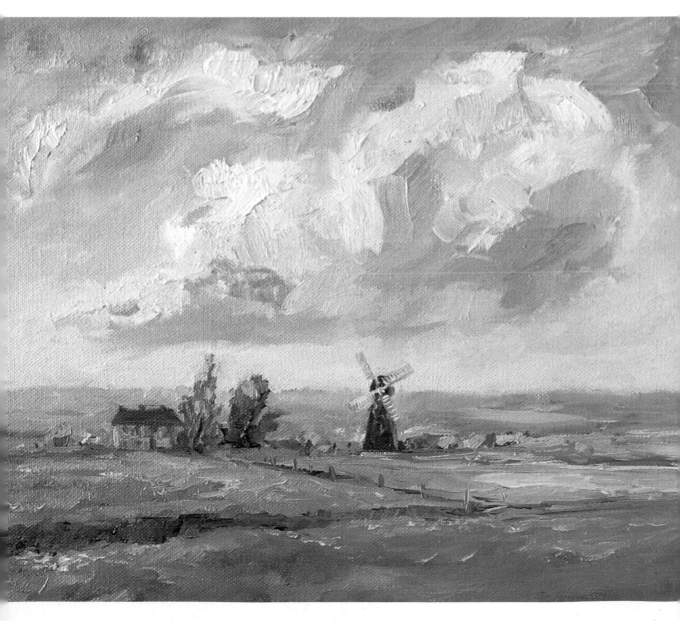

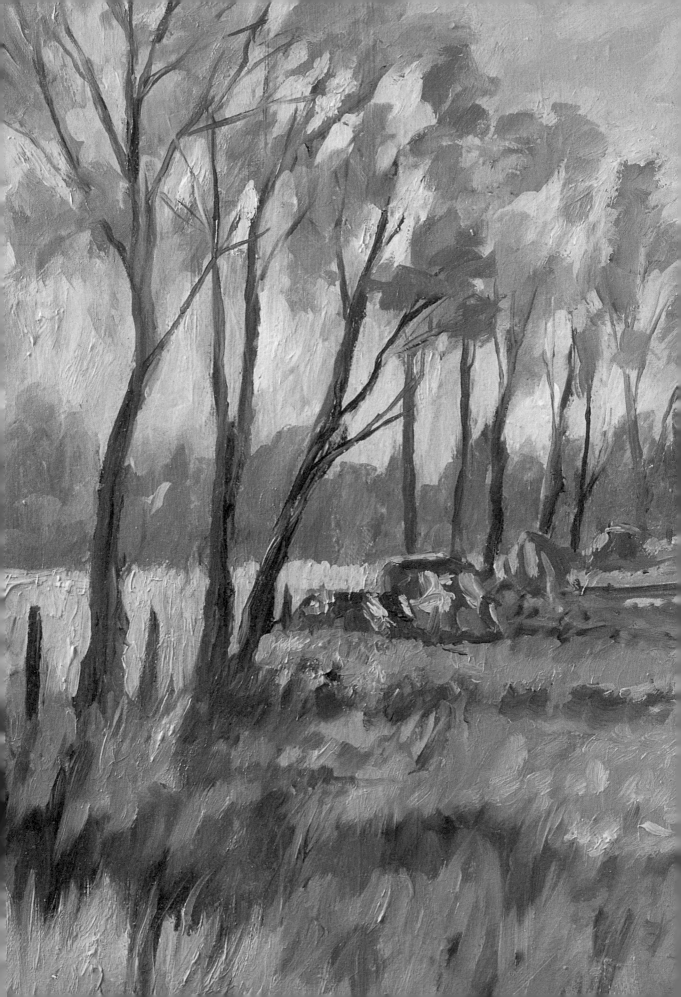

Trees for all Seasons

Trees are an integral part of the landscape. Not only do they grow in all shapes and sizes, but the colors vary greatly, starting with the full range of green shades in spring and summer, then changing to rich golds, reds, and oranges in the fall. Even in winter the bare branches of some varieties appear red, soft orange, or sometimes purple in the clear sunlight.

◀ **Ripley Watermeadows** (detail)
41 x 41 cm (16 x 16 in)

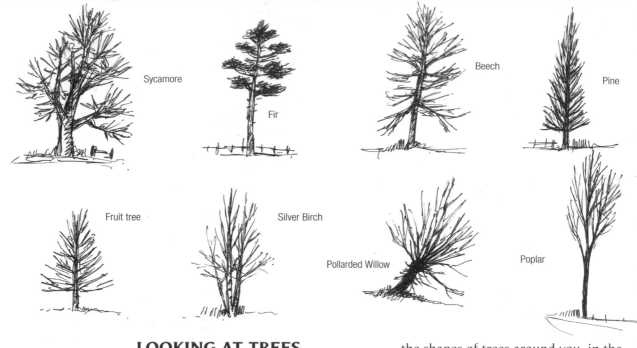

Sycamore

Fir

Beech

Pine

Fruit tree

Silver Birch

Pollarded Willow

Poplar

LOOKING AT TREES

In order to paint trees realistically, it is helpful first of all to learn a little about the structure of the different varieties. This is easiest in winter when most trees are bare of leaves. Start off by sketching the shapes of trees around you, in the garden or in al park. Make only small sketches and concentrate on getting the overall shape right, rather than capturing each branch. Remember, too, that even a simple painted sketch of a tree needs to

▶ **Clear Light, Romney Marsh**
10 x 12 in (25 x 31 cm)
This painting is a good example of how a single tree can provide the main point of interest in a composition.

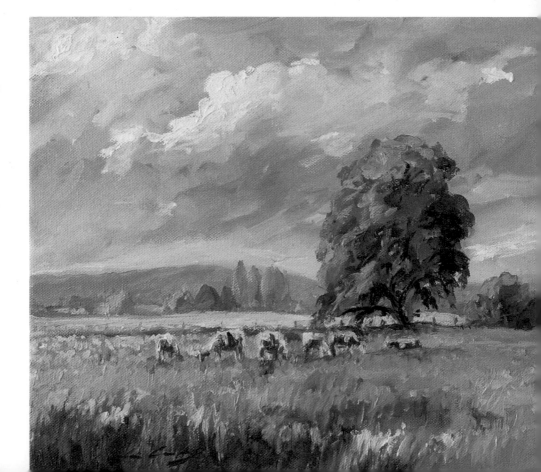

show its light and shadow sides. Use the tree sketches you have made to produce a series of small painted versions. To simplify the difference between the light and shadow sides, mix only two shades of green to start – viridian and light red for the dark tone, viridian and raw sienna for the lighter green. Block in the dark areas first of all – don't worry about the branches, just block in the basic shape. While the paint is still wet add the lighter areas on top, blending them together if you wish.

Distant trees and hedges

This basic light over dark technique is also ideal for depicting distant banks of trees and hedges, and, indeed, I make great use of this method in my paintings. Again, start off with a dark tone, blocking in the basic hedge shape, then adding highlights on top to create the finished hedge. Obviously this technique is only suited to far distant trees where details of branches and sky holes are not visible, but it is a simple way to start.

Another method for representing distant trees, particularly in misty conditions, is to paint their shapes almost in silhouette. To do this I mix up a warm gray tone and block in the top edge of the trees with a flat brush. Then I use the edge of the same brush to indicate a few main branches. Toward the base of the trees, I block in more flat shapes to add the impression of trunks. While working it is important to alter the gray tone slightly, making it a little darker for the trees closest to the viewer.

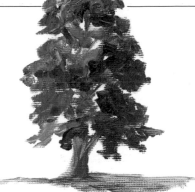

The lighter greens on the left-hand side and darker shadows on the right are the key to creating a realistic-looking tree in the middle distance.

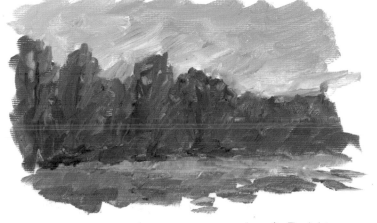

▲ The dark tones are blocked in first, then the highlights are painted on top to give shape to the hedgerow.

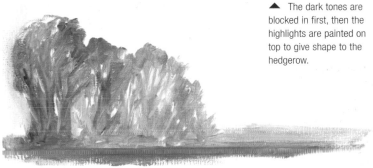

▲ Trees in the far distance have very little noticeable detail other than a suggestion of the main trunks and branches.

tips

◆ *Keep the initial dark tones fairly thin and add much thicker paint on top for the highlights.*

◆ *Unless a tree is in the foreground, keep details to a minimum. Individual leaves cannot easily be seen from 100 yards away.*

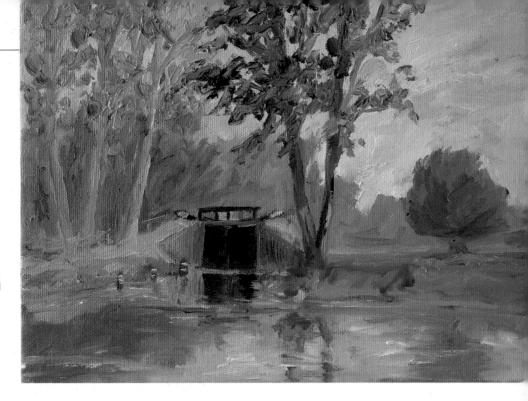

▶ **Below Newark Lock**
8 x 10 in (20 x 25 cm)
In this painting of Newark Lock
you can see trees painted in all
three distance planes, from the
bank of trees in the far
distance, with very little detail,
to the foreground trees where
individual branches and sky
holes are clearly visible.

▼ **Below Newark Lock**
(detail)
The sky holes have been
added last, applying the
paint very thickly in single
brushstrokes.

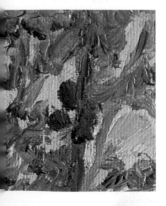

Foreground trees

As you look closely at individual trees
you will see much more detail, including
smaller branches and individual leaves,
although it is not necessary to paint
every leaf even when painting trees in
the foreground. Instead, try establishing
the main areas of color, light, and shade
within the overall tree and then look at
"sky holes," the shapes of individual
branches and clumps of foliage. Working
in this way you will show a considerable
amount of detail yet avoid painting
every leaf. This will keep your overall
painting looking impressionistic rather
than photographic in style.

"SKY HOLES" AND OTHER DETAILS

Usually when working in oils, it is easier
to paint the sky last. Where there is a
tree in the foreground of a painting,
however, a problem might be presented.
What if you have painted the tree first
and it is too solid? You will want to add

some openings in the foliage for the sky.

Before doing so, scrape off any excess
paint with a palette knife, though it will
not be possible to remove every trace of
green. When adding sky color, load the
brush with plenty of paint and place it
carefully, using a single brushstroke to
create each hole. This will enable you to
paint clean patches of light color over a
still wet area that was previously covered
with darker tones. If you try to blend the
paint, it will pick up any underlying
color and your sky will become muddy.
If this does happen, scrape off your
mistake with the palette knife and try
again – oils are very forgiving and will
enable you to do this several times.
Apply the sky color very thickly and
wipe off your brush after every stroke to
keep the color clean.

TRUNKS AND BRANCHES

Choosing the correct color for tree
trunks and branches also needs care.
Some trees, such as the silver birch, have

a very specific colored bark, but the color of all tree trunks and branches is affected by the light. Sometimes, when the sun is fairly low, tree trunks can stand out as very pale colors against their dark foliage. When seen against the light (that is, with light coming from behind them), most trunks and branches appear almost black. The only time branches appear to be their actual color is in flat, dull conditions.

COPING WITH SHADOWS

I am often asked by students, "what color is a shadow?" This, of course, depends upon the color of the object that is casting the shadow, but I have found that in landscape painting the shadow invariably contains a large amount of blue. When painting shadows cast by trees, I indicate all the shadows using French ultramarine on the wet underpainting unless I am working directly onto dry canvas. The wet paint blends easily and also picks up some of the underlying colors. Usually, I find that simply painting the shadows directly in blue is enough.

In particularly sunny conditions, not only are shadows cast by trees, but also the leaves of the tree may cast delicate shadows on the trunk itself – perhaps most noticeable on pollarded trees. These shadows need to be painted very softly; a darker tone of the tree trunk's own color usually works well. Otherwise, a soft gray tone mixed from cerulean blue and cadmium orange can also be used to successful effect.

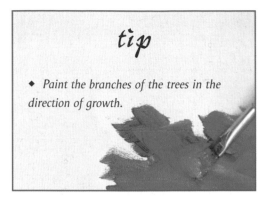

tip

◆ *Paint the branches of the trees in the direction of growth.*

▼ **First Snow, Riddlesdown**
10 x 12 in (25 x 31 cm)
The shadows on the lane were painted using pure French ultramarine, enabling the blue to pick up some of the underlying tones and creating clear, clean shadows.

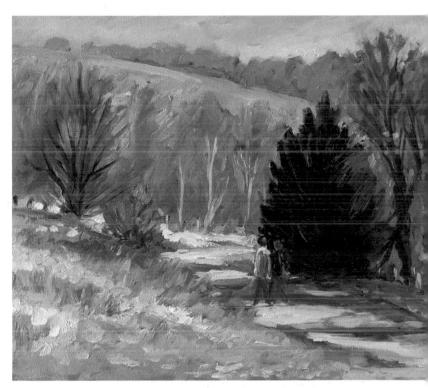

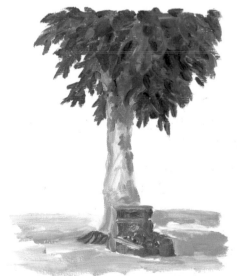

◀ The shadows on the top of the trunk of the tree have been painted using a soft gray tone mixed from cadmium orange, cerulean blue, and white.

THE CHANGING SEASONS

The colors of trees change with the seasons and, because they are such an integral part of the landscape, they have considerable impact on the finished painting.

Spring

In spring the new leaves bring fresh vibrant greens and yellows. These acidic green and yellow tones are exciting colors to paint. For the most impact, save the strongest tones for the foreground trees, toning down the colors in the middle ground by adding more cerulean blue to the green shades and a little white to make them paler. The presence of flowers in a field such as naturalized buttercups also helps to create the impression of a spring scene – just a few white or yellow stippled marks are often all that is needed.

Key colors for spring are lemon yellow, cadmium orange, cerulean blue, viridian, and raw sienna. Mix lemon yellow and cerulean blue to make a strong bright green that is the basis for the green of spring. Adding extra lemon yellow gives a bright acid tone, while cadmium orange produces a warmer green. Try using viridian as a base for dark greens, adding either cadmium orange or raw sienna to soften this very strong color.

▼ **Newark Lock**
10 x 12 in (25 x 31 cm)
The brightest spring greens have been reserved for the foreground trees. The contrast against the darker central tree adds extra interest to the picture.

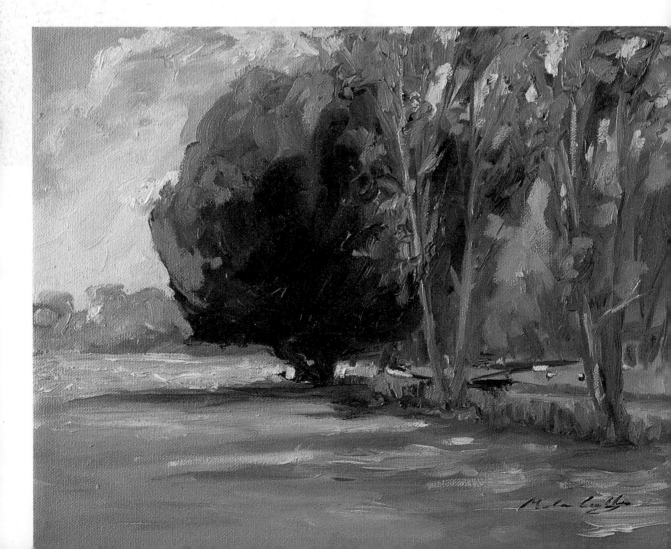

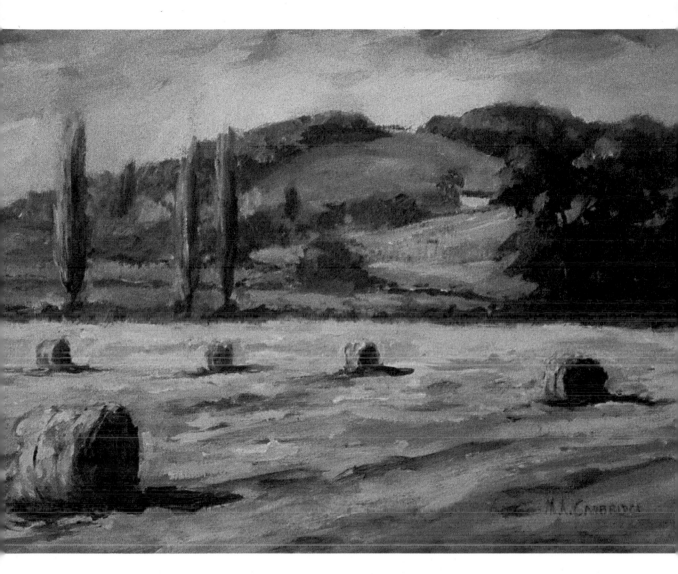

Summer

In spring woodlands offer a riot of bright greens and yellows for the oil painter, but in summer I prefer to concentrate on other landscape features such as fields and flower meadows, using trees as a setting rather than the main subject. This is because as spring moves into summer, greens tend to become somewhat duller and darker, forming a gentle background to the stronger golden yellows of wheat and other crops as they ripen. High summer can be a difficult time to paint trees since their green tones often seem dull and uninteresting, lacking the wide variety of color that is evident in either spring or fall.

The summer palette is dominated by darker greens and warm red tones: raw sienna, viridian, alizarin crimson, cadmium orange, light red, and French ultramarine. Use viridian as the base green, and add alizarin crimson for a very dark tone. Alternately, a little light red mixed with viridian makes a warmer, yet still dark, green. Both cadmium orange or raw sienna with viridian make good mid-tone greens.

▲ **Cornsilk**
12 x 16 in (30 x 41 cm)
As spring moves into summer, trees lose their initial brightness, becoming softer and bluer in tone, forming a beautiful backdrop to the strong yellows and golden shades of haystacks and ripening crops.

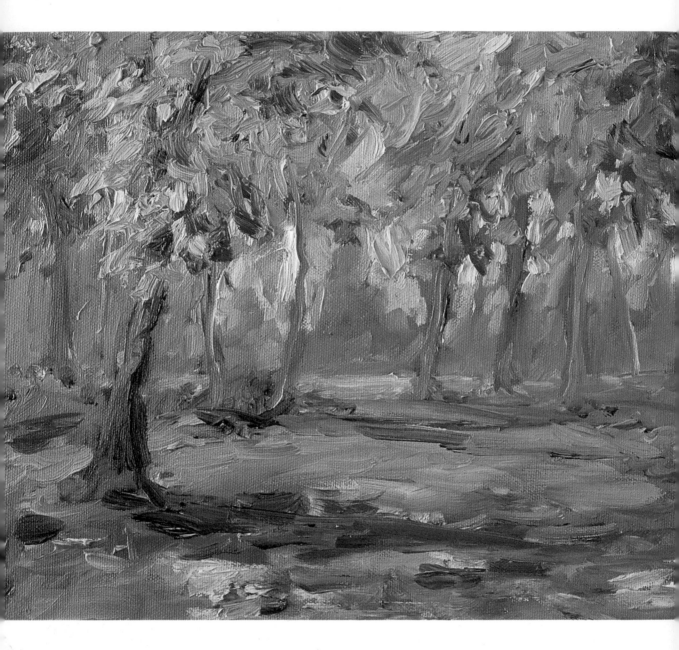

▲ **Fall Colors, Wisley**
10 x 12 in (25 x 31 cm)
Despite the use of many
strong fall colors, tones in
the middle ground have
been softened with a little
blue and white to keep a
sense of depth within this
woodland scene.

Fall

As fall arrives the greens turn gold,
bright yellow, or rusty orange, offering a
wonderful range of colors for the artist.
Beware, however, of making these colors
too strong in your paintings since they
can appear somewhat artificial.
Remember that the effect of the
intervening atmosphere will soften the
look of all colors, even for trees that are
only a few yards away from you.

Key colors veer toward a stronger,
brighter range: lemon yellow, cadmium
orange, light red, yellow ocher, and
viridian. Warm orange tones tend to
dominate fall trees, so try a mix of
cadmium orange and lemon yellow for
the brightest tones. Yellow ocher and
light red make superb darker orange
shades. Once again, try viridian with a
little cadmium orange or light red for the
darker shadow side of fall trees.

Winter

Winter brings its own reward for the artist, especially on a clear cold morning, when the range of colors is far wider than the expected subdued gray tones. Distant trees take on a purplish hue, with many warm orange tones visible. A number of trees and shrubs have strongly colored branches not normally seen when they are covered in leaves. In winter these shrubs are seen in their full glory, adding rich colors to the landscape. A snowfall also obviously has its own magic, highlighting some colors, especially in bright sunlight, and creating deep blue shadows as well.

These strong tones bring warm colors to the basic tree palette: alizarin crimson, cadmium orange, and light red, as well as cooler cerulean blue and French ultramarine. Use alizarin crimson and French ultramarine for the darkest purple shades. Light red and French ultramarine give a warm black for tree trunks and some branches. Use cadmium orange and cerulean blue with white to mix a whole range of warm and cool grays (see page 24).

▼ **Winter Snow, North Downs**
12 x 16 in (31 x 41 cm)
Snow is rarely pure white, even on sunny days. Note how dark the foreground snow appears when compared to the white of the surrounding page.

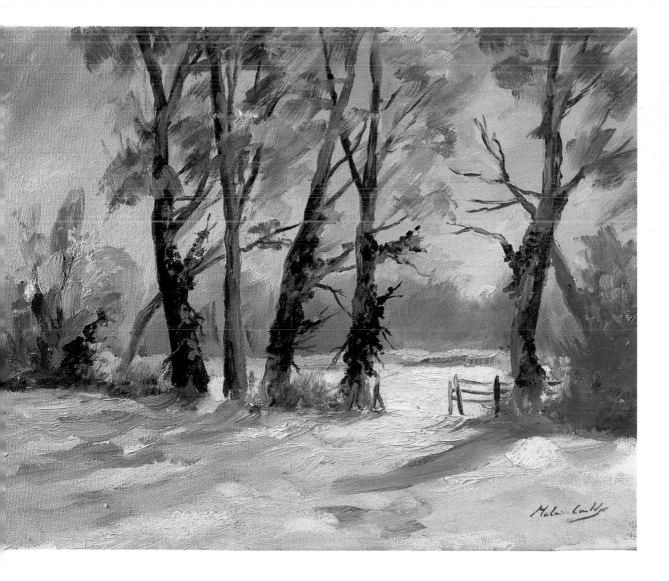

demonstration
Summer Haystacks

Late summer is a wonderful time for painting. The fields turn to gold as wheat and barley ripen, and there is often a blue haze to distant hillsides. In my painting I have tried to concentrate on the color and simplicity of the scene, treating the haystacks as simple blocks and looking at the trees in the background as areas of different color rather than painting the individual leaves.

you will need

canvas 12 x 16 in (30 x 40 cm) (primed with acrylic burnt sienna)
brushes: No. 10 short flat, No. 8 short flat, No. 4 rigger

colors

titanium white, lemon yellow, cadmium yellow deep, raw sienna, light red, alizarin crimson, cerulean blue, and French ultramarine.

tips

♦ *Work directly over the wet paint using lively, short brushstrokes to give a sense of movement.*

♦ *Do not clean your brush while painting the field; the mixture of colors helps create a textured effect. Small patches of raw sienna also help to give a feeling of depth toward the foreground.*

♦ *Do not clean your brush until the whole sky is finished. If necessary, wipe off any excess blue paint with a clean rag.*

♦ *When painting the sky holes, apply a large amount of paint in one brushstroke to prevent the underlying color showing through.*

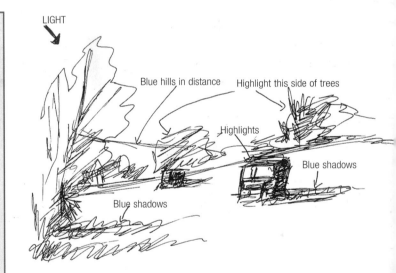

LIGHT

Blue hills in distance

Highlight this side of trees

Highlights

Blue shadows

Blue shadows

▲ **STEP ONE**

Wherever possible, I try to work from a sketch made on location rather than a photograph. My sketch for *Summer Haystacks* is covered with color notes and arrows indicating areas of light and shade. Particularly note the large arrow in the top left-hand corner, indicating the direction of sunlight on the scene.

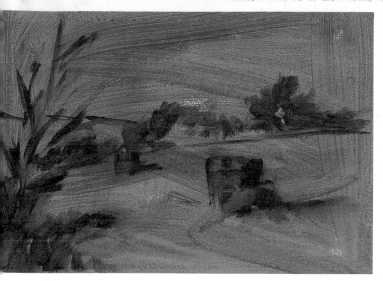

◀ STEP TWO

Before starting the painting, I primed the canvas with a wash of acrylic burnt sienna. Having a colored ground to work on enables the artist to see both the lightest and darkest tones immediately. With a No. 8 flat brush loaded with French ultramarine, I sketched in the key areas of the painting.

STEP THREE

...used French ultramarine and white to paint ...e distant hillside. Then I mixed lemon ...ellow and cerulean blue for a bright green ...nd I added French ultramarine for a darker ...ade. With the dark green, I painted a line ...f lively brushmarks for the shadows along ...e hedgerow, then finished with the lighter ...reen. I began painting the field using a No. ...0 flat brush with mixtures of yellows. The ...ft-hand tree was blocked in using raw ...enna and cadmium yellow for the sunlit ...de, with light red added for the shadow.

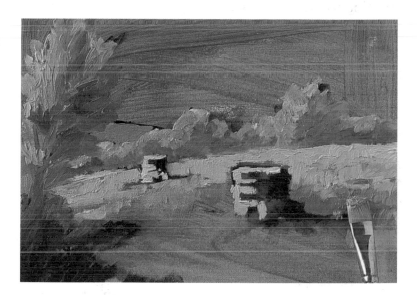

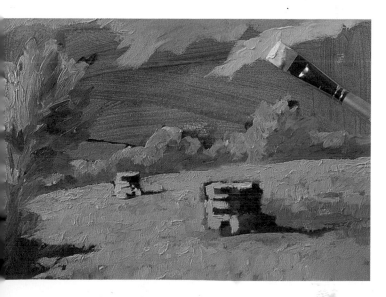

◀ STEP FOUR

I continued painting the field with a No. 10 flat brush, holding the brush upright and using short downward brushstrokes to create the stubble texture. Then I turned to the sky, starting at the top of the canvas with the strongest blue mixed from cerulean and white. Using fast, scrubby, brushstrokes, I blocked in the top of the sky, adding more white with a little cadmium yellow for the tops of the clouds. Shadows on the clouds were mixed from alizarin crimson, cerulean blue, and white.

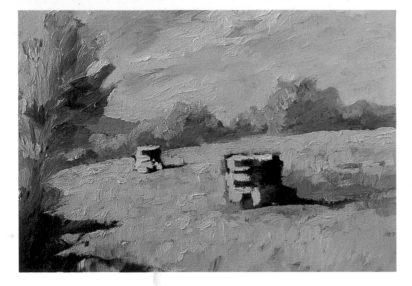

◀ STEP FIVE

I finished painting the whole sky area using the same approach and making sure that the color graduated from light blue at the top, becoming warm yellow in the middle, and changing to a pinkish yellow at the horizon.

▶ STEP SIX

With the whole canvas now covered in paint, it was time to put in the details and bring the painting to life. Using a No. 8 flat brush, I painted the haystacks. These are simple cube shapes, created using short vertical and horizontal brushstrokes. I used cadmium yellow and raw sienna but added French ultramarine for the shadow side of the haystacks and for the shadows created by the left-hand tree.

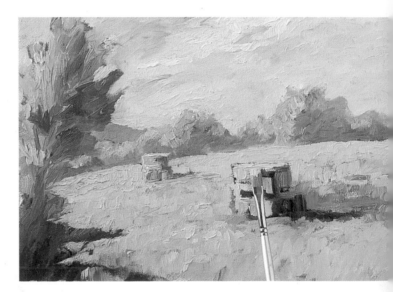

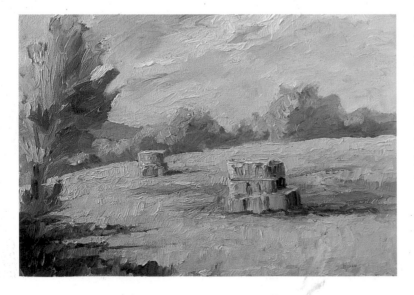

◀ STEP SEVEN

The yellow field of stubble appeared too bright in the foreground, so I softened this with a little cerulean blue applied directly over the yellow with a No. 10 flat brush. I used only light pressure on the brush to avoid picking up too much underlying yellow. Shadows from the haystacks and the left-hand tree were strengthened using French ultramarine and light red.

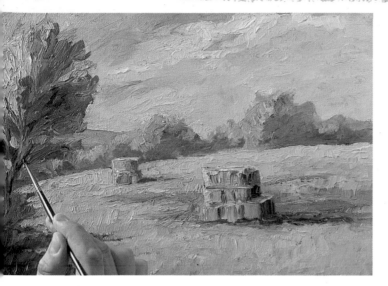

◀ **STEP EIGHT**

Branches in the foreground tree could now be painted using a No. 4 rigger brush with a mix of French ultramarine and light red. Finally (*see below*), I painted sky holes into the top quarter of the tree using a No. 8 flat brush, heavily loaded with the sky mixture of cerulean blue and white.

▼ **Summer Haystacks** 12 x 16 in (30 x 40 cm)

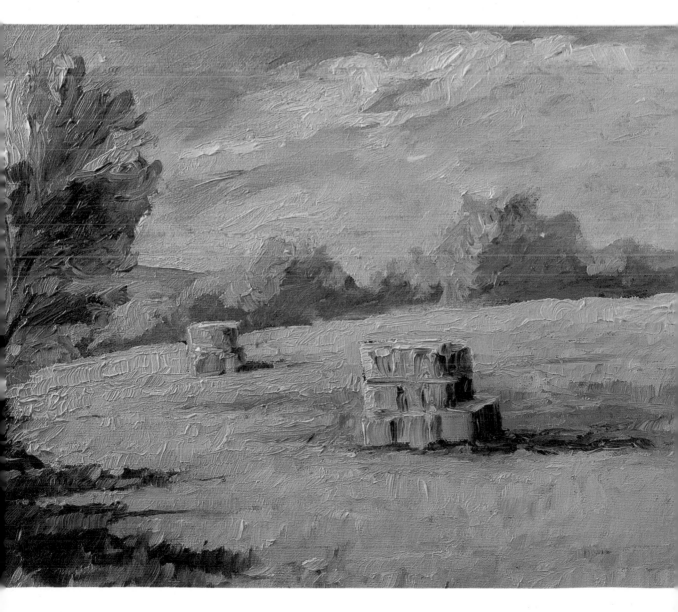

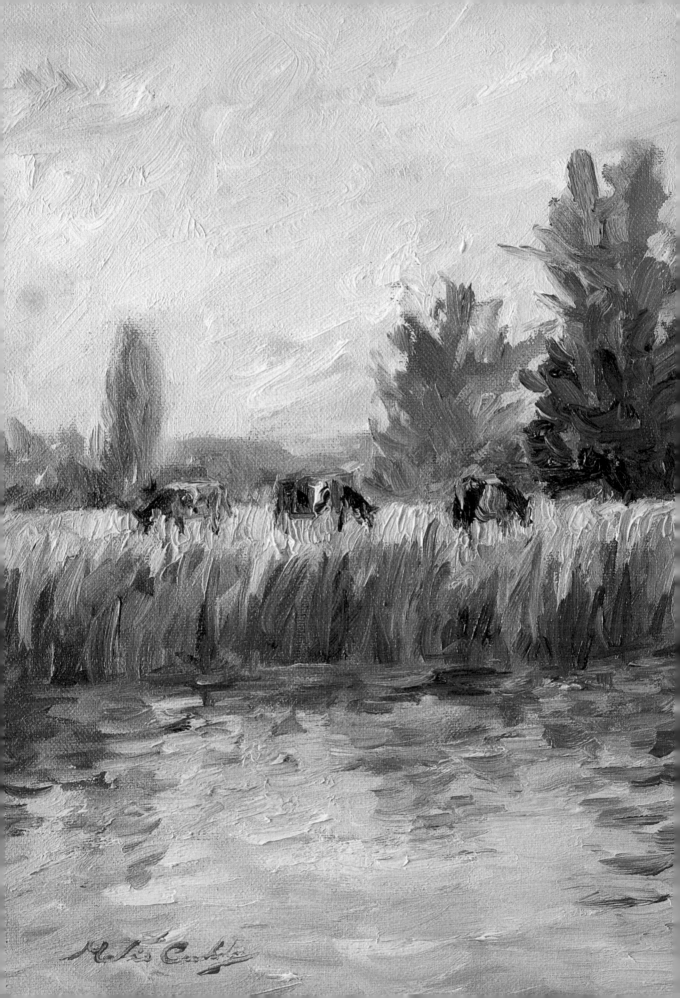

Water and Reflections

Gaining the skill and confidence to paint water opens up a range of popular subjects for the artist – quiet rivers, lakes, and even the open sea, not to mention waves crashing onto the beach. By sticking to a few simple rules and following the practical examples in this chapter you will start to gain confidence when you are faced with a scene containing water, whether it's moving or still.

STILL WATER

Painting water with oils should be very straightforward. The fact that oil paint can be worked directly on top of wet underpainting is a definite advantage. Colors slightly blend together automatically, without any real effort from the artist.

Reflections

Reflections in calm water are probably the easiest way to depict water in a painting. But there are a few points to bear in mind. Reflected colors tend to become slightly duller and have less detail. This is because of the degree of clarity of the water itself – for example, the water in a still pond may be full of algae or sediment and this will affect the reflected colors. Even the slightest breeze across water causes tiny ripples that will distort a reflection.

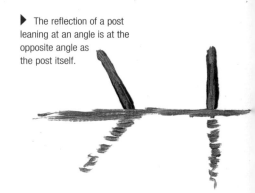

▶ The reflection of a post leaning at an angle is at the opposite angle as the post itself.

Another key point to be aware of is the size of the reflection. For instance, when painting the mast of a moored yacht, the reflection is often longer than the actual mast, particularly in very calm water. Remember, also, to take into account the angle of the reflection.

Adding ripples

Before considering more complicated scenarios, try painting a simple still water reflection with just a few ripples breaking the surface. Keep the pressure

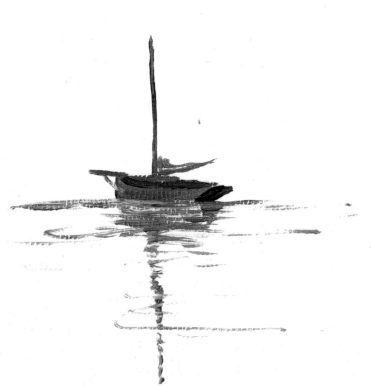

▼ Reflections in a moving surface appear rather distorted. However, unless the water is very rough, the reflection of the mast of a boat is still at least as tall as the actual mast.

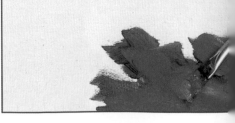

tips

◆ Remember to add just a little of the complementary color, red, to dull down the green tones for the reflections.

◆ Use shorter brushstrokes fairly close together for ripples in the foreground. Several longer lines will be sufficient for the middle and background.

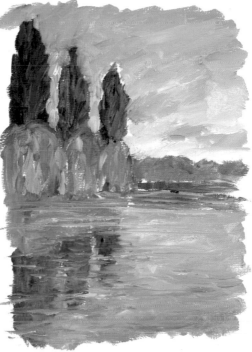

Start by painting the reflection, using downward brushstrokes only. Concentrate on getting each color in the right place and approximately the right shape. Patches of sky also appear slightly darker in tone, so these areas should be blended toward the bottom of the reflection, ensuring that the whole area of water is covered with softly blended oil paint. Add the surface ripples in a series of short horizontal brushstrokes with a No. 4 round brush.

▼ **Fishing Hut on the Charente**
20 x 16 in (51 x 41 cm)

f your brush fairly light in order to void the brush picking up too much nderlying color. If you find that the olors are becoming muddy, try painting e ripples with a lot more paint to give most an impasto effect. Clean your rush after each brushstroke to remove ny undercolor picked up and to keep e highlights and ripples clean.

Vorking wet-into-wet

ne great advantage of depicting water ith oils is the ability to work wet-into-et, even painting on consecutive days, us allowing plenty of time to get the flection right before moving on to add e surface ripples. Painting the ripples rectly onto the wet reflection means at some of the underlying color will picked up by the brush and the pples will blend themselves slightly to this wet surface, becoming a part of e water rather than merely sitting on p of the painting.

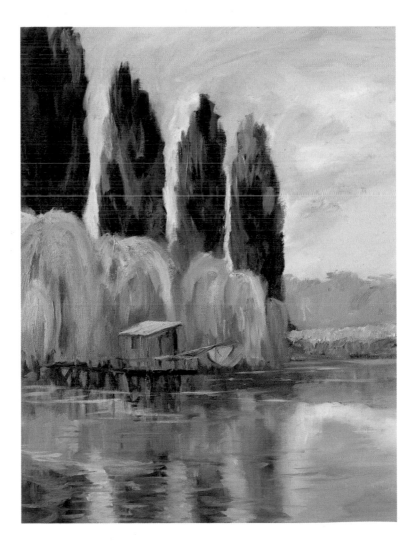

MOVING WATER

When painting rivers and lakes, the technique is fairly similar. Capturing the colors and movement of the ocean when painting at the seacoast requires a somewhat different approach, however. To start with, the sea is seldom calm enough to cause mirror-like reflections. Its color is probably most influenced by the sky above, while the amount of movement and the size of the waves are governed by the effect of the prevailing winds.

In deep water the sea tends to reflect the darker blues from the sky, often appearing very dark blue toward the horizon. Use French ultramarine with a little cadmium orange, but no white, for this wonderful dark sea blue. Similarly, bands of dark green are sometimes seen in this part of the sea where clouds cast shadows on the surface. Use a combination of French ultramarine and viridian for the darkest greens, adding a little raw sienna to make them lighter if required. Moving forward toward the shore, the sea is much shallower and its color is affected by the beach, appearing first as a paler green, which can be mixed from cerulean blue and yellow ocher.

▼ **The Blue Yacht, Porchester**
11 x 14 in (28 x 36 cm)
In this view across Portsmouth Harbor the distant water was quite choppy. I used short horizontal brushstrokes for the waves and painted flatter areas of color in the foreground where the water was calmer.

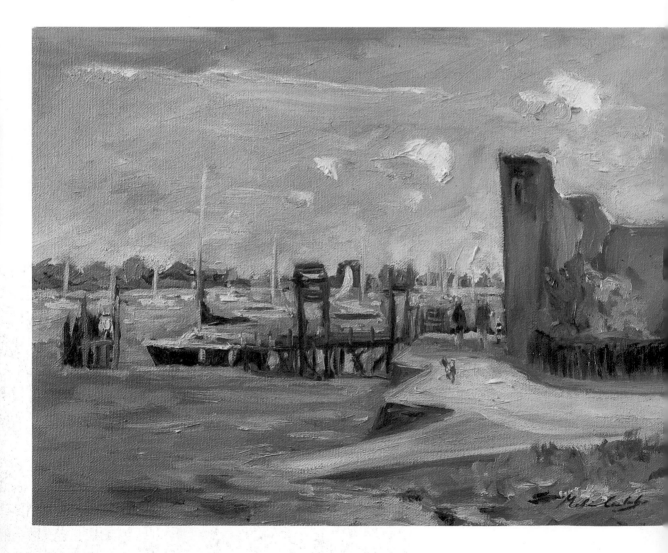

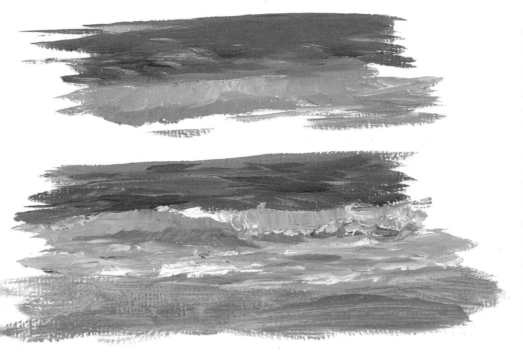

◀ Sweep a mix of blues across the paper for the sea on the horizon. Moving down, paint a greenish stripe under the dark blue, finishing off with a very yellowish band to form the back of the breaking wave.

◀ Use white with a little raw sienn for the foam of the breaker. A few vertical brushstrokes give the effect of falling water, with dabs of cream for the breaking surf. Check that the shadow under the foam is dark enough. Add squiggles to represent foam patterns on the shallow water creeping up the beach. Finally, indicate the beach with a little raw sienna.

becomes almost yellow where the waves break and pick up sand deposits, so more yellow ocher or a little lemon yellow should be added to the prevous mixture for this final shade. These sea colors are obviously only a guide, but use them for a sound starting point.

Simplifying waves

While some artists devote all of their efforts to painting the open sea, most only paint the sea as part of a beach scene. Waves break onto the shore in a fairly standard way, so by learning how to paint one wave you will have the key to success!

Beach reflections

Unlike reflections in still water, reflections on a beach are usually only found in the wet sand and, even here, they are distorted, requiring a somewhat different approach in painting. Rather than paint the reflections first using

downward brushstrokes, incorporate them into the painting of the beach itself using mainly horizontal brushstrokes.

To paint beach reflections accurately, the key is to not attempt to be accurate. For example, the reflection of a figure with a white T-shirt and green shorts would simply be a long squiggle of skin tone followed by a stroke of green and a slightly larger one of white. Finally, add another small skin tone mark.

▼ **Surf's Up, Polzeath Bay**
20 x 24 in (51 x 61 cm)
In December when I painted this, there were plenty of breakers at Polzeath Bay. I included several lengths of surf to give the impression of the rough incoming sea breaking onto the beach.

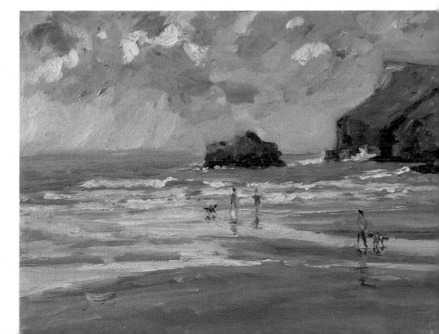

demonstration
The Thames at Bourne End

This tranquil view of the River Thames with drifting sailing dinghies near Bourne End made an irresistible subject. The water was calm enough to show the long reflections from the sails of the dinghies, yet parts of the surface were covered in ripples from the flow of the river. I particularly liked the contrast of white sails against the dark trees and wanted to make this the key element in my finished painting.

you will need

canvas 12 x 18 in (30 x 45 cm) (primed with acrylic burnt sienna)
brushes: No. 8 short flat, No. 4 round, No. 4 rigger, No. 10 short flat

colors

French ultramarine, cadmium orange, raw sienna, viridian, cerulean blue, alizarin crimson, and titanium white.

tips

• *Let the brushstrokes create the impression of trees by working in different directions to give a three-dimensional effect.*

• *Paint the reflections using downward brushstrokes only, blending to give a smooth surface.*

• *Reflected sky tones should be just a little darker than the actual sky.*

• *Use very light pressure on the brush when adding reflections and wipe the brush after each stroke over the canvas to prevent it picking up too much underlying color.*

• *Balance the composition by painting the foreground reflections of the trees and dinghies off the bottom edge of the canvas.*

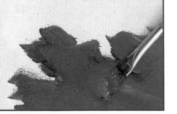

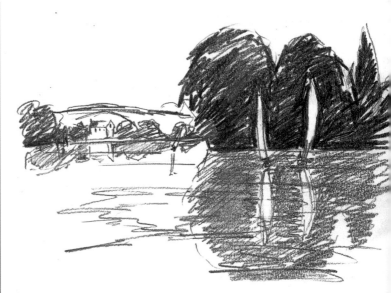

▲ **STEP ONE**

My initial drawing of the scene concentrated on the overall composition and position of the two dinghies in the foreground. The reflections of the dinghies have also been drawn in – note how they are slightly longer than the height of the actual sails.

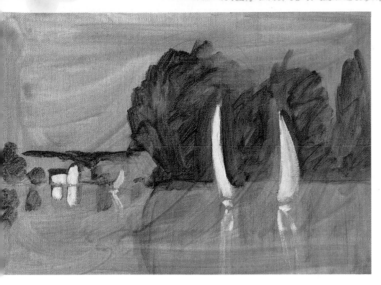

◀ **STEP TWO**

Working on a canvas tinted with a thin wash of acrylic burnt sienna, I blocked in the main composition using French ultramarine and a No. 8 flat brush. Note how the trees on the right have been painted as solid shapes. The dinghies and distant house were also blocked in at this initial stage, using pure white. To balance the composition, reflections of the two boats go off the edge of the bottom of the canvas.

STEP THREE

I started to paint the far hillside using a No. 8 flat brush loaded with viridian, French ultramarine, and white. In front of the hillside is a bank of trees running down to the water's edge, and I used the same mixture of colors, but with less white and a little raw sienna for these. With the same color on the brush, I marked in the reflections of these trees. This was done by holding the brush flat to the canvas and dragging down at least as far as the height of the trees.

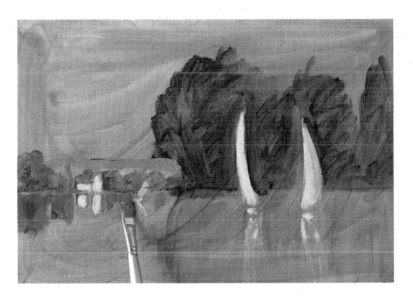

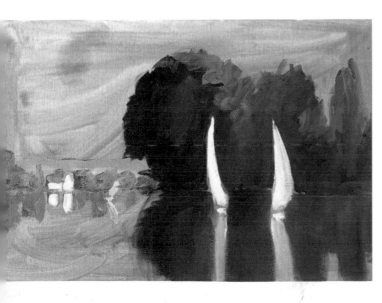

◀ **STEP FOUR**

Using a No. 10 flat brush, I strengthened the initial shapes of the foreground trees on the right-hand side with a mixture of viridian and a little French ultramarine first, then with raw sienna added for the lighter tones, and cadmium orange for the darks. I concentrated on the overall shape of each tree. At the same time, using downward strokes, I painted the reflections of the trees to the bottom of the canvas. A little space was left for the sky tones to reflect between the two poplar trees on the far right.

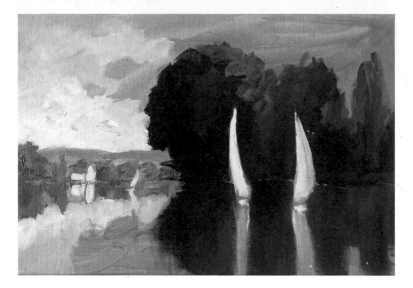

◀ **STEP FIVE**

Now I could paint the sky and its reflection. Using the No. 10 flat brush, I started at the top with the darkest blue tone mixed from cerulean blue and white with a little French ultramarine. Keeping the brushstrokes fairly fluid, I painted down toward the horizon, adding white to lighten the color and finally adding a little cadmium orange near the horizon. While working on the sky I added sky tone to the water reflections using the same brush, but applying the paint evenly with blended downward-only brushstrokes.

▶ **STEP SIX**

I continued painting the sky and its reflection until all the canvas was covered with paint. The water reflections were now finished and only the ripples remained to be added. Before doing this, however, the foreground trees needed to be brought to life. I added sky holes to the top of these trees, using plenty of sky color and wiping the brush after each brushstroke. Next I used a No. 4 rigger to paint the tree trunks and branches with raw sienna. Finally, texture was added to the trees using viridian and raw sienna.

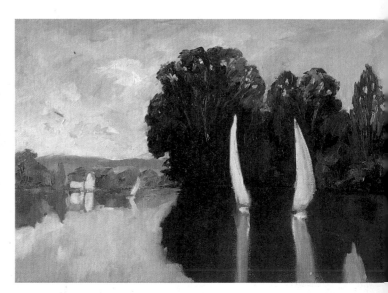

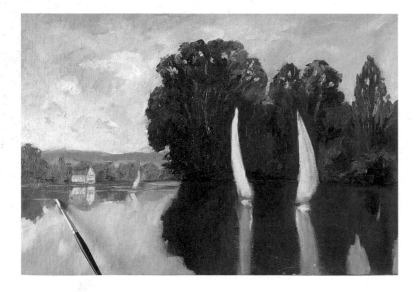

◀ **STEP SEVEN**

Painting the surface ripples is an easy and enjoyable process. I started with a No. 4 round brush loaded with a pale gray tone mixed from cerulean blue, cadmium orange and white. Holding the brush at a gentle angle, I drew in a few horizontal lines over the reflection of the distant hillside. It is best to work slowly at this stage and to try to keep these lines as horizontal as possible, using a mahlstick if you prefer.

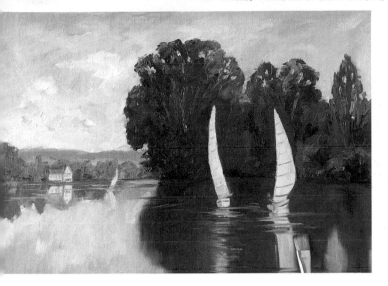

◀ **STEP EIGHT**

A red stripe was added to the hulls of the two dinghies and a figure painted into the right-hand boat. For the foreground ripples I used a clean No. 10 flat brush. I held it vertically so that the edge just touched the wet paint and gently dragged it from the white sail reflections into the dark tree reflections. To complete the painting (*see below*), I continued to work slowly, blending the pale reflections across into the darker areas.

▼ **The Thames at Bourne End** 12 x 18 in (30 x 45 cm)

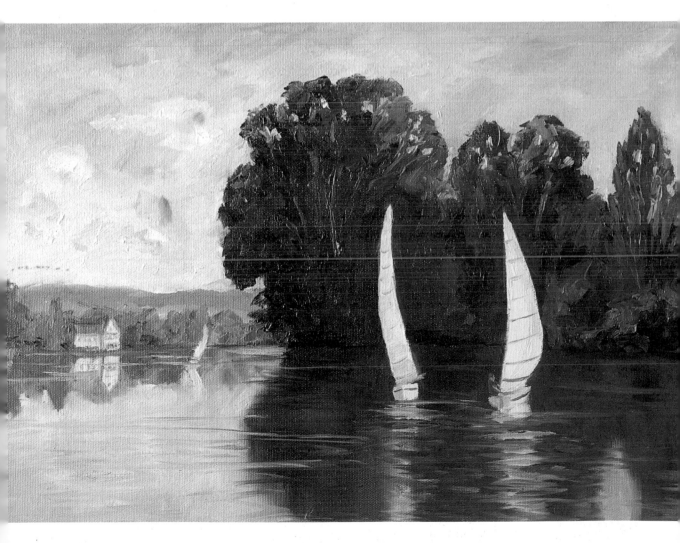

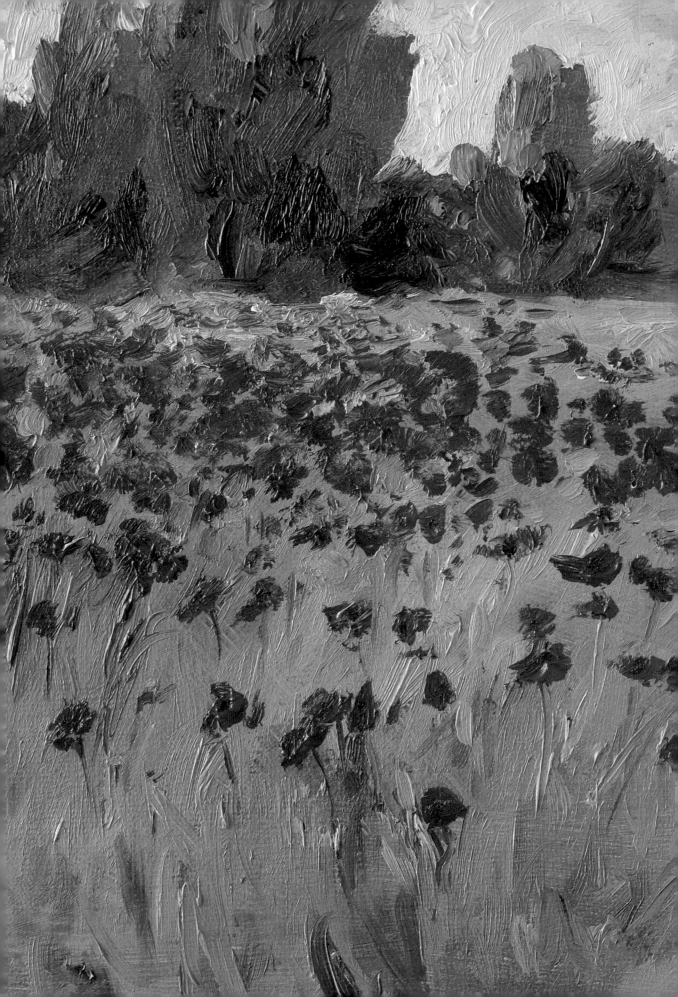

Flowers in the Landscape

For an artist, discovering a landscape filled with flowers is a particular joy. Whether a dappled carpet of bluebells in an English woodland in springtime, a field of ripening sunflowers in Provence dazzling in the afternoon light of late summer, or the view of a meadow covered with poppies near my home – all of these sights make me want to paint.

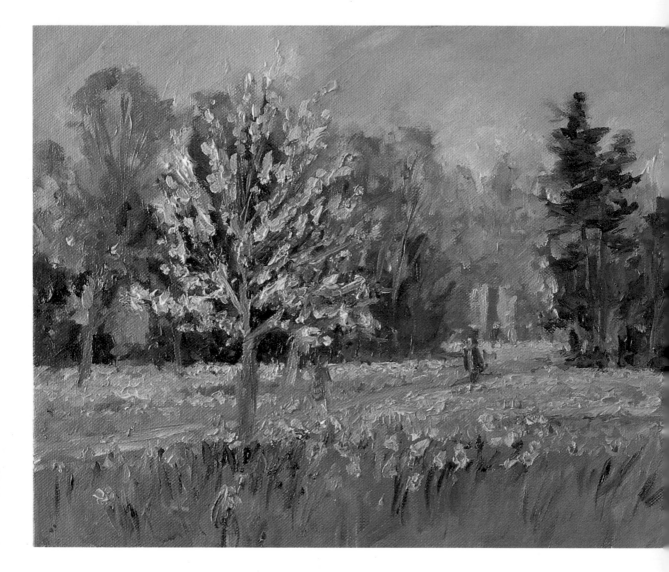

▲ Springtime, Hampton
Court Gardens
10 x 12 in (25 x 31 cm)
A display of daffodils en
masse makes an irresistible
subject. Here, only the
foreground flowers are
painted in full. I used
splashes of yellow and
white among the green
meadow to give the
impression of flowers
receding into the distance.

LOOKING AT FLOWERS

Flowers thrive in many different
environments allowing the artist to
feature them in many kinds of paintings,
from a simple still life to a riot of color in
a garden. The following pages concentrate
on a few kinds of flowers that you are
likely to come across in the open
landscape and show how to incorporate
them into a successful composition.

Planning compositions

It is easy to become completely enchanted
by the flowers themselves with little
thought to the composition of the whole
painting. When flowers are a part of a
landscape, it is particularly important to
make sure that they look as though they
belong within the context of the painting
rather than as elements added at the end.
When you first sit down to paint a
landscape containing flowers, the key
question to ask is, "Do I want the flowers
to dominate the whole painting or to be
subtle extra?" As you will see from the
compositional sketches shown here, both
ideas work well, provided you plan a little
at the beginning.

◀ Here the sunflowers dominate the scene, with the background church adding a focal point.

Individual flowers

Before you begin including flowers in your landscape paintings, it is helpful to look more closely at flowers that are familiar to you that you will probably see in the countryside. Keeping a flower sketchbook can be very helpful by providing a useful source of ideas for the future. Sketches need not necessarily be in oils; simple pencil notes or watercolor sketches will be just as valuable as reference.

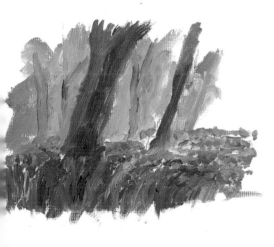

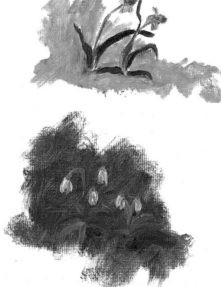

◀ Springtime flower studies

POPPIES

The shape of the poppy flower is fairly simple, usually having six overlapping petals and leaves that grow straight out from the main flower stem. When seen in a meadow only the vibrant red flower heads or purplish seed pods appear from among the grasses. This makes them fairly easy to paint, and since these colorful flowers need very little detail to make them look realistic, they are ideal for the beginner.

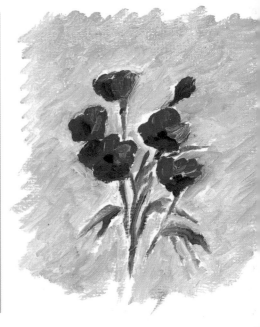

exercise

Copy the poppy study (right). Mix a little alizarin crimson with cadmium orange to create a bright red for the flower shape, add a little cerulean blue for the highlights and use alizarin crimson on its own for the darker petals. Paint the central dark blotch using a mix of French ultramarine and light red. The three-pronged leaves are viridian and raw sienna for the dark tone, with viridian and lemon yellow for the brighter green.

▼ **The White House**
8 x 10 in (20 x 25 cm)
The whole meadow was painted first and the poppies added last with single brushstrokes of pure red tones. The flower centers were indicated where they could be seen, and the poppy stems blended into the wet color of the meadow. This helped keep the red colors vibrant. A sense of distance was created by painting larger flower heads in the foreground.

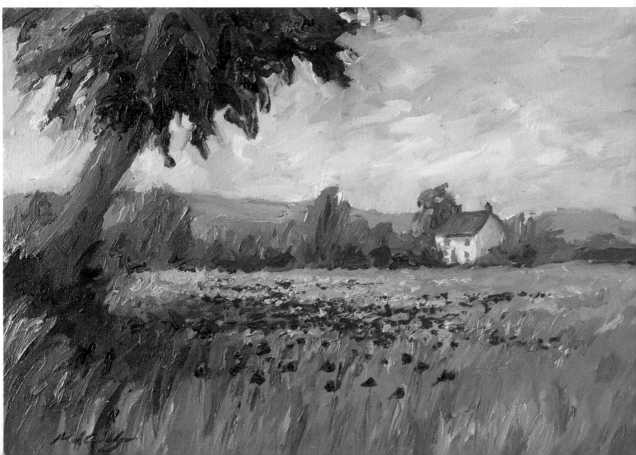

BLUEBELLS

Bluebells are a particularly English phenomenon, and the best time to visit a bluebell wood is during April when the flowers should be at their very best. The carpet of blue and purple under a light canopy of fresh green leaves is an absolute delight to any artist.

Getting the color to look realistic for bluebells, however, is not easy. Contrary to popular belief, they are not really blue – more a blend of purple, pink, and blue. To achieve a natural-looking color, mix several different shades of blue, using French ultramarine, alizarin crimson, and white, and paint the flowers using all of these colors. The key point to remember is that all the bell-shaped flowers hang from one side of the stem, bending the stem itself over in a curve. Leaves are a soft gray-green shade (mix viridian with French ultramarine and white for these) and are long and thin, rather like grass stalks.

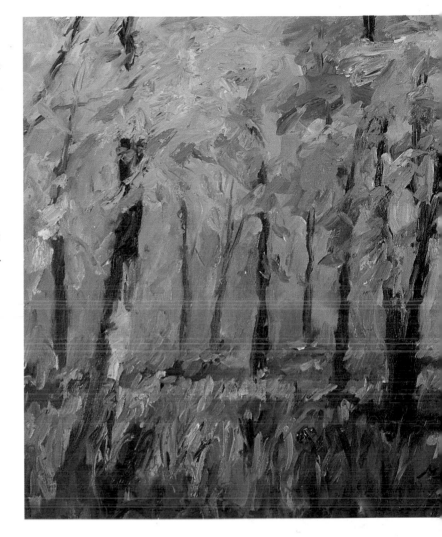

▲ **Kingswood Bluebells**
41 x 41 cm (16 x 16 in)
In a woodland scene such as this it is difficult to distinguish individual flower heads but very obvious if the overall blue shade is not quite right. I used a blend of French ultramarine, alizarin crimson, and cerulean blue with some white for my bluebell colors.

When incorporating bluebells into a woodland scene, concentrate on getting the color right, and remember to vary the blue shades to create the effect of sunlight filtering through the trees above. Only the flowers in the foreground will need to show individual bell flower shapes; further back in the woodland a blend of colors can create the impression of flowers rather than giving too much detail.

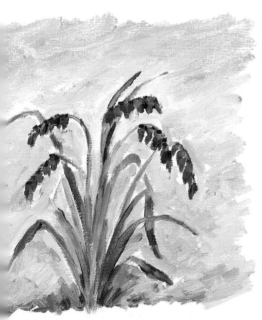

◄ **Bluebells**

LAVENDER

Lavender crops provide another interesting flower-based subject for painting. In much warmer climates, lavender is grown as a commercial crop rather than as a garden flower.

The lavender is usually grown in individual clumps that look like a line of giant purple-backed hedgehogs. Look first at a single clump of lavender to observe the flower; tiny bud-like flowers

▼ Lavender

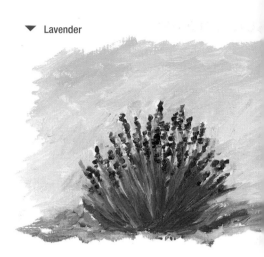

▼ **Lavender**
16 x 12 in (41 x 30 cm)
This painting of lavender growing near Sisteron in Provence, France, captures the atmosphere of the flowers without showing detail. Individual flowers are only seen in the foreground, with dabs of color creating the impression of more flowers further back.

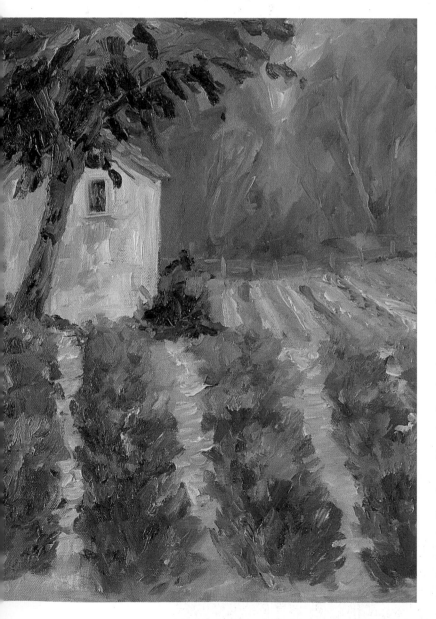

are clustered at the top of fine stems. Leaves are gray-green in color, thin and spiky. To paint a clump of lavender, start off with a mixture of viridian, French ultramarine, and white. Paint the basic overall shape with a No. 4 flat brush, remembering to create spikes toward the edges. Lighter green stems can be added to one side with a fine round brush and little lemon yellow added to the mixture Create each flower with a series of dots from the top of the flower stems downward using the same brush and a dark purple mixed from French ultramarine and alizarin crimson. The purple shade can be lightened with white to add a few highlights to some flowers to bring them to life, concentrating particularly on those flowers on the same side as the lighter green stems.

When painting the earth in between the rows of lavender, try a mix of raw sienna, cadmium orange, and white for the basic earth color. Add brushstrokes of pure cerulean blue on top of this wet paint for subtle shadows and also to add texture.

SUNFLOWERS

Sunflowers are one of my favorite subjects for painting. They are also particularly easy to paint in oils and so form the basis for the demonstration on pages 80–83. Once again, you will first of all need to consider the basic structure and colors.

In early summer the flower heads appear with small dark yellow centers. As the season moves on the heads begin to ripen, turning much darker and swelling as they do so. By September the flower heads look much larger with dark brown/blackish centers, making a wonderful contrast to the bright yellow outer petals. Leaves are mid green to gray-green in color on thick stalks.

It is a good idea to select and mix all the colors you will need before you actually start painting. You will need several yellow shades for the petals – pure lemon yellow, pure cadmium yellow, and raw sienna . French ultramarine mixed with light red makes a good dark tone for the centers of the

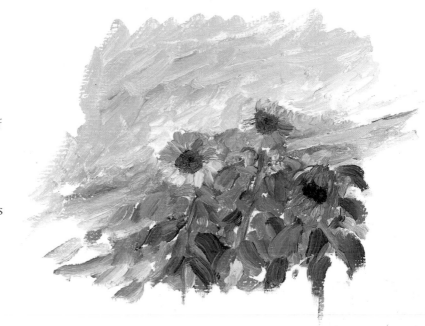

▲ Sunflowers

flowers. Try a basic mixture of lemon yellow and cerulean blue for the leaves.

Several circular shapes are painted for the centers of the flower heads, using a No. 4 flat brush loaded with a dark, almost black tone. The petals are added using both lemon and cadmium yellows. Use single brushstrokes from the center outward to create each individual petal. Leaves are also single brushmarks linked together with thin lines for the stems.

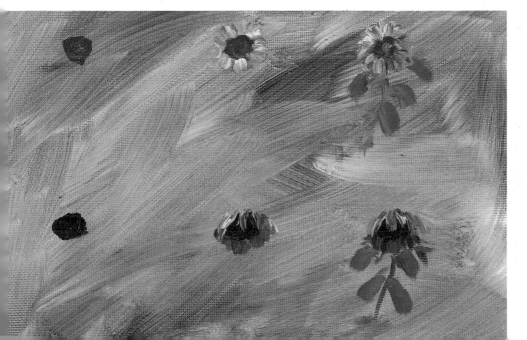

◀ The technique for painting individual sunflower heads whether facing the sun or bending over is the same. Start with the flower center, adding yellow petals all the way around. Sunflower heads are large, so remember to add some darker petals at the bottom using raw sienna to show petals shaded by those at the top of the flower. Then paint the main leaves and stem.

demonstration
Sunflowers near Benon

Sunflowers ripening in the late summer heat are such a delight to paint. In order to create the shimmering effect of a field of sunflowers in the breeze, I chose to paint on a thin wash of alizarin crimson. This cool pink shade provides an excellent contrast to the warm yellow tones of the flowers themselves. A sense of scale and receding distance are important elements in this painting.

you will need

canvas 10 x 12 in (25 x 30 cm) (primed with acrylic alizarin crimson)
brushes: No. 8 short flat, No. 4 short flat, No. 4 round, No. 10 short flat

colors

French ultramarine, light red, cadmium orange, yellow ocher, lemon yellow, cadmium yellow deep, raw sienna , cerulean blue , viridian, and titanium white.

tips

♦ Form the actual flowers from the texture of the brushstrokes.

♦ Allow some of the pink underpainting to show through in places to help create a sense of movement.

♦ Create a sense of distance by including much more detail in the flower heads of the first two rows, but reducing these details so that they become a series of abstract brushmarks towards the horizon.

♦ Paint the sky before starting to paint the sunflowers. This makes it easier to judge the yellow tones rather than having too much pink underpainting still visible.

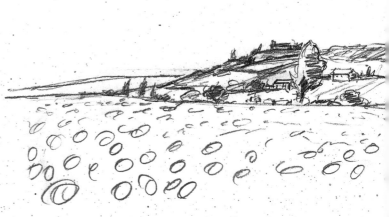

▲ **STEP ONE**

My initial sketch set out the background hillside and buildings to establish the basic composition. The pattern of sunflowers is roughly indicated with a series of circles. Note how the first two rows of flower heads are much larger than those further back to create a sense of scale within the sunflower field, helping it to recede into the distance.

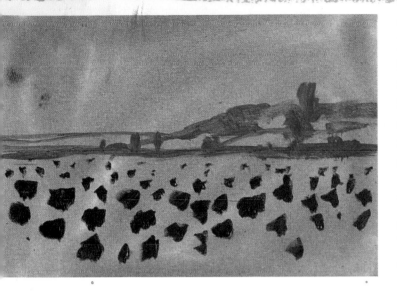

◀ STEP TWO

First I primed the canvas with a thin wash of acrylic alizarin crimson and allowed this to dry. Using French ultramarine and a No. 8 flat brush, I painted in the horizon line and distant hillside, making sure that the tree on the right-hand side broke through the top of the hill. This set the scale for the background. Flower heads were painted as simple dots of light red and French ultramarine at this stage, but I made the foreground flower heads much larger than those further back to create a sense of distance.

▶ STEP THREE

Next I painted the far hillside using French ultramarine grayed down with cadmium orange and white. Greens for the middle hill were a mix of viridian and yellow ocher with some cerulean blue added. The buildings were painted with a No. 4 flat brush, using yellow ocher, cadmium orange, and white.

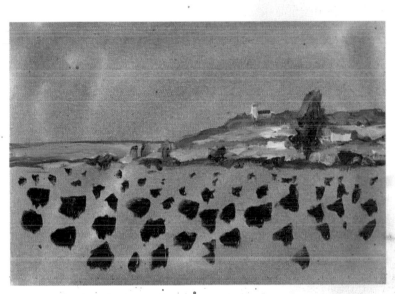

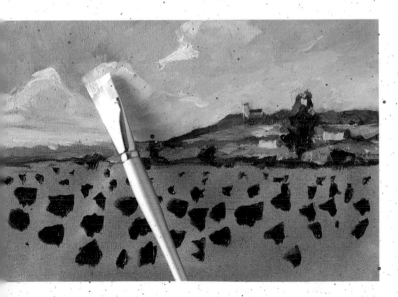

◀ STEP FOUR

After establishing the horizon line and middle distance hillside, I was ready to paint the sky. I used a No. 10 flat brush and a mixture of French ultramarine and cerulean blue at the top and added white further down. Clouds were painted using cerulean blue, cadmium orange, and white, keeping the brushstrokes loose and being careful not to paint a hard edge around each cloud. I added a very thick highlight, using white with a little cadmium orange, to the top of each cloud, and soften the darker bottom edge with my finger.

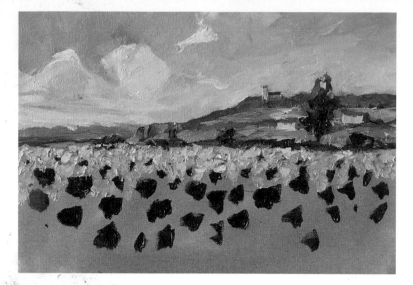

◀ STEP FIVE

Using a No. 8 brush with lemon yellow and white, I marked in random dots and small brushmarks for the top of the sunflower field. Actual flowers are not visible when they are far in the distance. I mixed lemon yellow, cerulean blue, and white for a soft pale green and added a few more dots in between the yellow ones for the leaves.

▶ STEP SIX

I used a No. 4 flat brush turned on its edge to paint the flower petals. I started with the shadow petals at the bottom using raw sienna, then added the lighter petals, using lemon and cadmium yellow deep. The middle hillside now appeared too dark, so I used a bright green and lemon yellow to overpaint the hedgerow and main tree on the right-hand side, using a No. 8 flat brush. Windows and doorways on the buildings were added with a No. 4 round brush, using the same gray as for the distant hill.

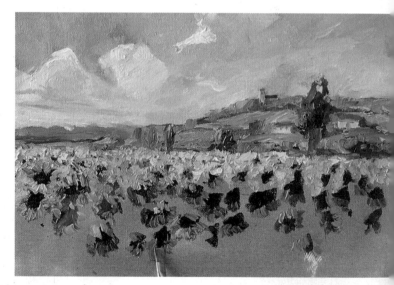

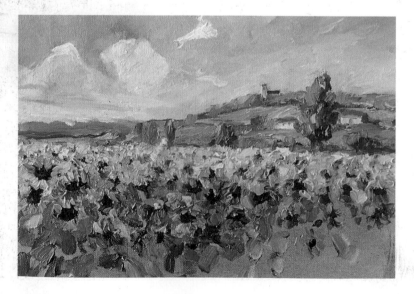

◀ STEP SEVEN

Once I had painted flower petals around all the dark heads, I used a No. 8 flat brush to add more leaves in between the flowers and toward the bottom of the canvas. Each leaf was produced by a single directional brushstroke, helping to create an overall impression of movement rather than an abundance of detail. Finally, I left plenty of unpainted canvas toward the bottom of the picture to paint in foreground earth.

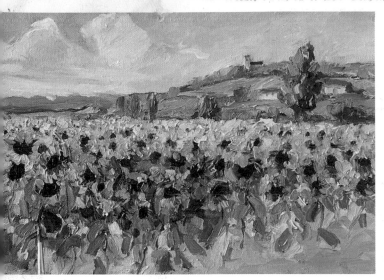

◀ STEP EIGHT

I used a No. 8 flat brush and loose brushstrokes to paint the earth. Raw sienna and white formed the basic tone, with a little cerulean blue added for shadow. With a No. 4 round brush I defined some of the foreground leaves and added a few stems to the front row of sunflowers. Finally (*see below*), I re-painted any of the sunflower centers and petals that had become obscured.

▼ **Sunflowers near Benon** 10 x 12 in (25 x 30 cm)

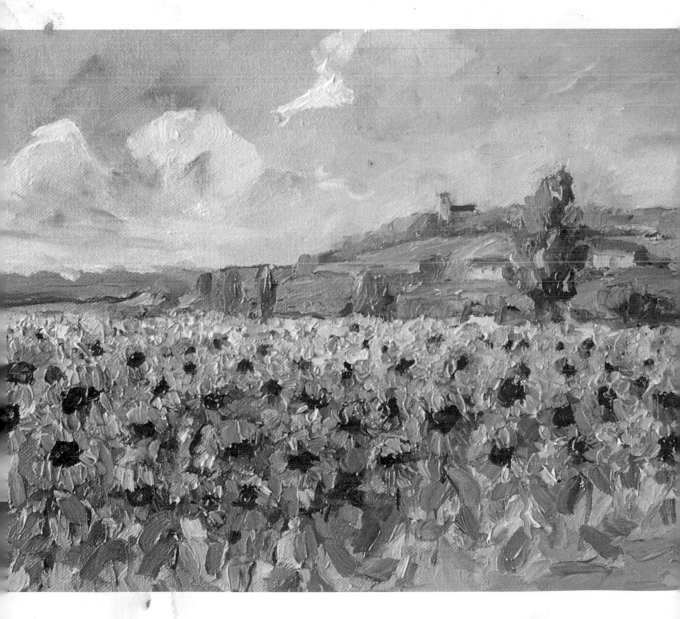

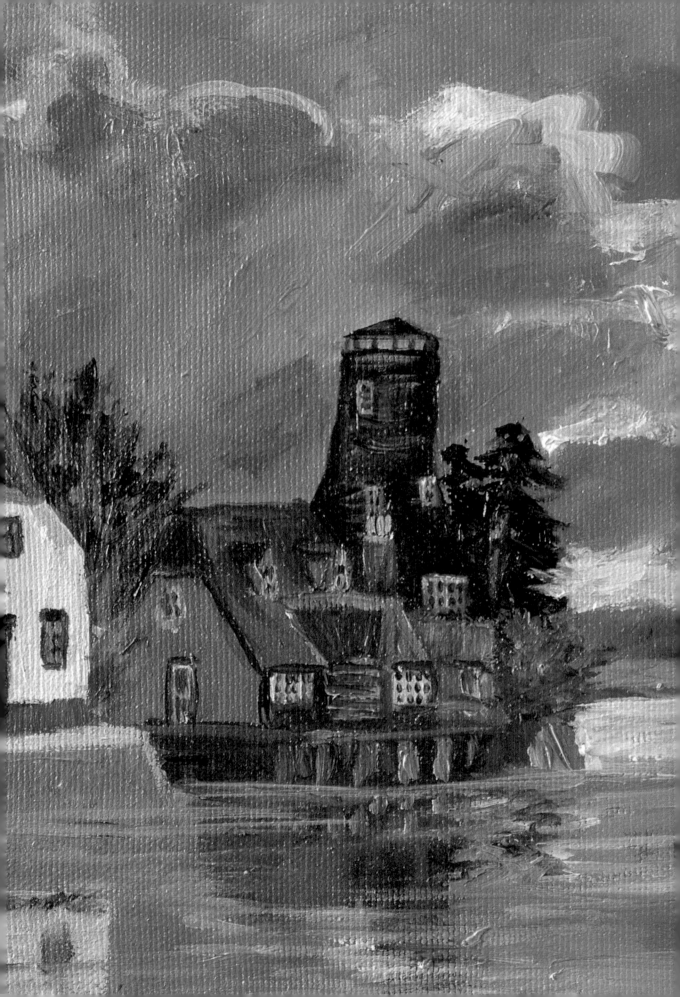

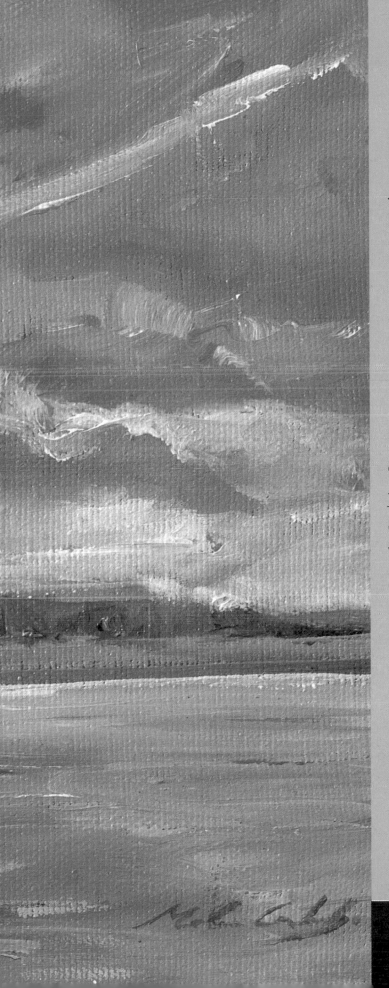

Buildings
in the
Landscape

Buildings are an integral part
of many landscapes, so it is to
your advantage to feel
confident in painting them.
While there are some points
of perspective to bear in
mind, an understanding of
basic shapes and proportion
will help you to simplify the
subject. Using these simple
methods of measurement
will enable you to tackle
buildings even if you find line
drawings difficult.

◀ **Watermill at Langstone**
20 x 25 cm (8 x 10 in)

► Start by painting a basic square shape. Then darken the red with a little viridian, or the complementary of whatever color you have chosen, and paint the side. Finally, use your lightest tone to paint the top and complete the cube.

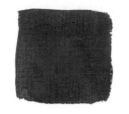

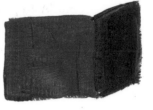

WORKING WITH CUBES

Most buildings are made up in reality of a series of block shapes, so start by painting these rather than worrying too much about the outlines. By breaking down each building into these blocks and other shapes, it is possible to build up the finished shape from within. This approach of building with paint rather than relying on a basic outline is the key to painting many complex objects successfully.

Most students will recognize the basic cube. A cube or rectangular shape, along with other shapes, can be used to create a building, a church for example. This simple method will help you approach buildings that are to be painted in the middle distance which do not require much detail.

► Using flat shapes, take a little raw sienna and paint a tall rectangle for the church tower, placing a horizontal rectangle alongside it for the actual church. The roof shape is painted with a gray tone mixed from French ultramarine, cadmium orange, and white.

► The tower looks three-dimensional with a thinner flat shape alongside (white added to raw sienna). Windows are single brushstrokes in a darker mixture of the roof gray. A line of darker gray along the edge of the roof indicates the shadow of the overhanging tiles.

BASIC MEASURING

Another important element in painting a successful building is the correct scale in proportion to the rest of the landscape. This can be achieved using a simple pencil measurement. First hold a pencil at arm's length between thumb and forefinger. Look along the pencil at your chosen subject and pick out a "key measurement" (maybe the side of a building or a handy telephone pole). Use your thumb to mark the measurement on the pencil.

Having established a single base unit of measurement, use this to compare other aspects of the building; for instance, the length of the barn is two units, the wall is one and a half units,

etc. With practice you may find you can dispense with careful measuring by pencil because using your eye will become enough.

tip

◆ *While measuring, also check the angle of each line in relation to either the horizon line or vertical edge of the page.*

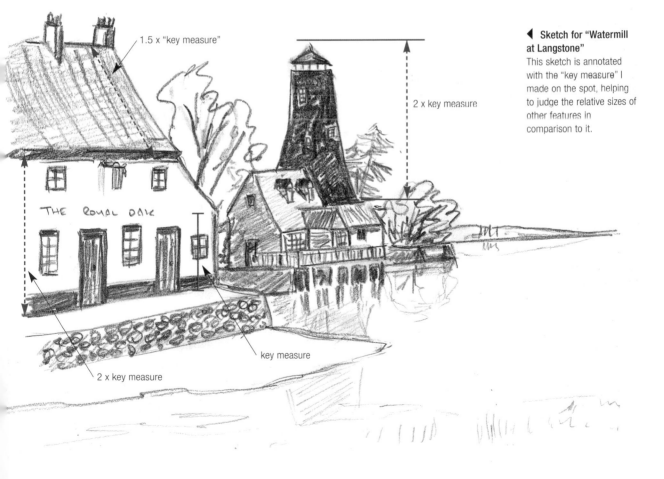

1.5 x "key measure"

THE ROYAL OAK

2 x key measure

key measure

2 x key measure

◀ **Sketch for "Watermill at Langstone"**
This sketch is annotated with the "key measure" I made on the spot, helping to judge the relative sizes of other features in comparison to it.

GROUPS OF BUILDINGS

Moving on from painting a single simple building to painting a whole street or village should not change the initial approach. The overall subject may seem more complicated, but by starting with block shapes, then adding details such as chimneys and windows, the whole street can often be treated as a single building.

▼ Start by painting the basic block shapes, concentrating on the main walls and roof angles.

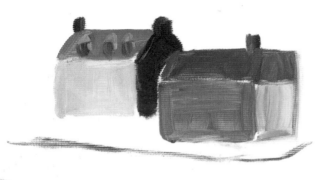

WINDOWS, DOORWAYS AND OTHER DETAILS

Windows, doorways, and chimneys show the character of a building, particularly an old or historic one. Getting these details correct guarantees your finished painting will look right. In my view of *Brasted Tea Rooms* the windows are of different sizes and at different levels, particularly on the first floor. This is not a mistake; they actually were like that! Observation of such detail is important; the offset windows give the impression of an old cottage shop – exactly what the building was.

Unless you are working on a large scale, most building details will probably be less than 1 in (2.5 cm) high in your paintings. Windows need only be a dark

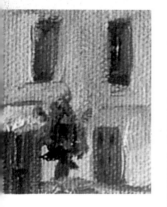

▲ **Brasted Tea Rooms**
(detail)
The windows were first painted in a dark tone. Then paler window frames were added on top using a No. 4 round brush.

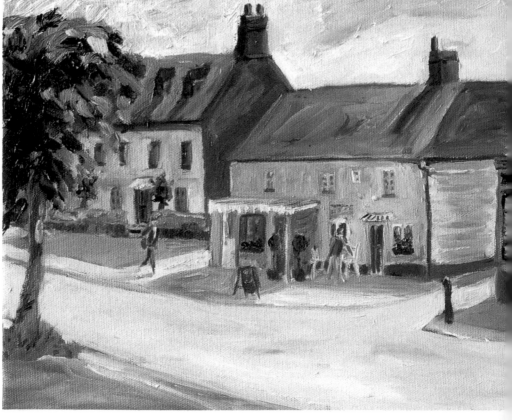

▶ **Brasted Tea Rooms**
25 x 31 cm (10 x 12 in)

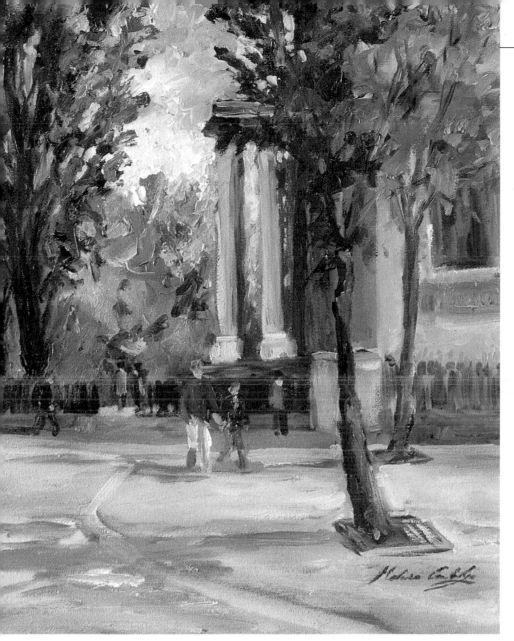

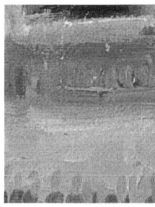

◀ **Behind St Paul's**
12 x 10 in (31 x 25 cm()
This view of St Paul's Cathedral was painted on location in fairly cold, windy conditions. Note how the foreground figures add a sense of scale.

▼ Details on the stonework were kept to a minimum, using a mixture of yellow ocher, cerulean blue, and white.

ctangle, with paler lines indicating the amework. Doorways are also painted as nall blocks, using an initial dark tone; rench ultramarine and light red make a ood starting point. I used this method paint the cottage windows and door r *Brasted Tea Rooms*.

When painting the stonework on *ehind St Paul's* I used the individual rushmarks to create the textures around e main window, varying the strength of olor to add extra interest. A No. 4 flat rush was ideal for this purpose.

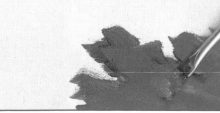

tip

◆ *When painting white features, tone down pure white with a little French ultramarine. In this way you can reserve pure white (or even white with a touch of lemon yellow added) for the highlights.*

demonstration
Roussillon, France

Incorporating buildings into a landscape can be a daunting prospect. In this painting of a French village at Roussillon, perched high on the famous red/ocher cliffs, the village forms the focal point, but because it is in the middle ground, the buildings can be reduced to simple block shapes, and details can be added later. The final result is a successful painting, produced with very simple techniques.

you will need

canvas 14 x 16 in (35 x 40 cm) (primed with acrylic burnt sienna)
brushes: No. 8 short flat, No. 4 short flat, No. 4 round, No. 10 short flat

colors

French ultramarine, light red, cadmium orange, yellow ocher, viridian, cerulean blue, alizarin crimson, and titanium white.

tips

◆ *Paint the whole wall of each building with a single brushstroke if possible.*

◆ *Paint the cliffs with loose brushstrokes, working in different directions to give an impression of texture to the rocks.*

◆ *Make sure the shadow sides of each building reflect light coming from the top right of the canvas.*

◆ *Windows should be slightly darker than the surrounding building colors.*

◆ *Add shutters to some windows to give some individuality to different buildings.*

◆ *Don't forget to paint the chimneys.*

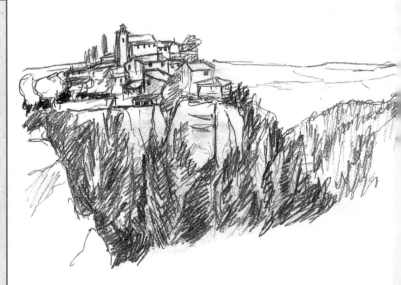

▲ **STEP ONE**

This view across the valley toward Roussillon was sketched during a vacation. Having parked the car for a few moments, there was just time to note down the basic composition, writing down a few notes on the side to remind me of the brilliant colors of the red cliffs and dark shadows in the forest below.

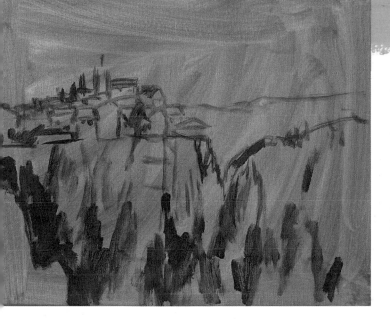

◀ STEP TWO

I primed my canvas with a thin wash of acrylic burnt sienna. Then I sketched in the basic composition with a No. 8 flat brush using French ultramarine. The buildings are indicated with simple outlines, while the foreground trees are blocked in as flat blue tones. These trees would form the darkest area of the finished painting.

STEP THREE

ill using the No. 8 flat brush, I painted in
e buildings as basic block shapes. I started
ith a mixture of cadmium orange and
hite for the lightest sides of the buildings,
en added French ultramarine to this
ixture for the shadow sides. I painted roofs
 each building in the village using the same
chnique, but this time with a mixture of
dmium orange and yellow ocher for the
ghter roofs, and light red and French
tramarine for the darker shadow sides.

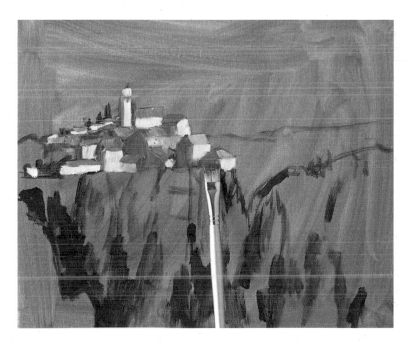

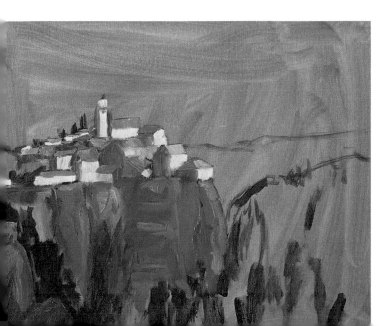

◀ STEP FOUR

Next I blocked in the cliffs. I used light red and French ultramarine for the basic cliff tone, but added cadmium orange and yellow ocher for the lighter tones. The foreground rock face was also painted at the same time. In a picture like this it is important to make sure that the middle cliffs are a little paler than those in the front left-hand corner in order to create a sense of distance.

▶ **STEP FIVE**

I blocked in the background hills, starting with the hills furthest away and using a soft gray mix of French ultramarine and cadmium orange with plenty of white. Then I blended in a little extra French ultramarine and viridian to create the impression of a distant forest. For the second hillside, I added viridian and yellow ocher to the original gray mixture for a stronger green. I created the conical tops of the trees with the edge of the No. 8 flat brush.

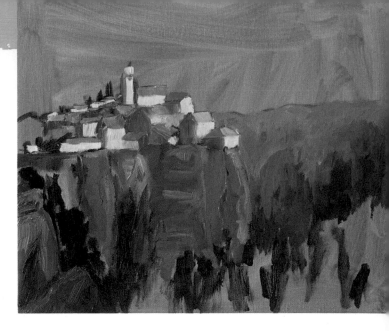

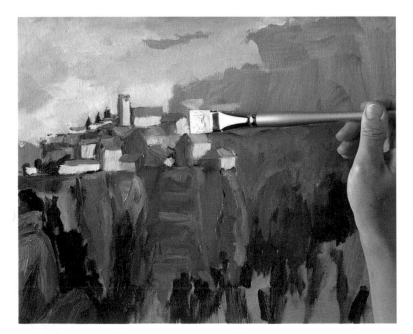

◀ **STEP SIX**

Now, I could paint the sky. I used a No. 10 fl[at] brush, starting at the top of the canvas, with [a] mixture of French ultramarine, cerulean blu[e] and white. The effect I wanted was produce[d] with soft brushstrokes, blended by working fairly rapidly. As I painted toward the horizo[n] I added more white and a little cadmium orange to the mixture and used the sharp edge of the flat brush to paint right up to th[e] edges of the buildings.

▶ **STEP SEVEN**

Once the sky was complete I could add windows and other details to the buildings. I used French ultramarine grayed down with cadmium orange and applied the paint with a No. 4 round brush. I painted each window as a single line initially and remembered to put a shadow line under the eaves on some of the roofs. Shutters for some of the windows were also produced with a single sideways brushmark, using a No. 4 flat brush.

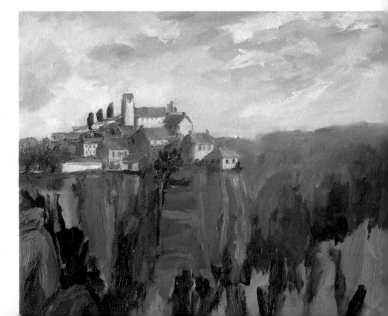

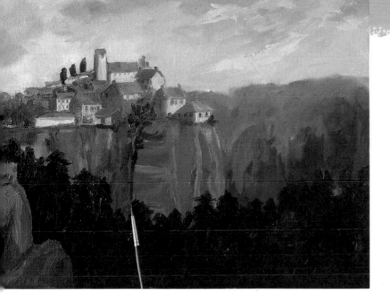

◀ STEP EIGHT

I blocked in the foreground trees using viridian and alizarin crimson for the darkest greens, and added yellow ocher for the lighter tones, then painted the feathery tree tops. Finally (*see below*), I painted the tree trunks with light red and yellow ocher, and added two figures under the trees to the far left of the village.

▼ **Roussillon, France** 14 x 16 in (35 x 40 cm)

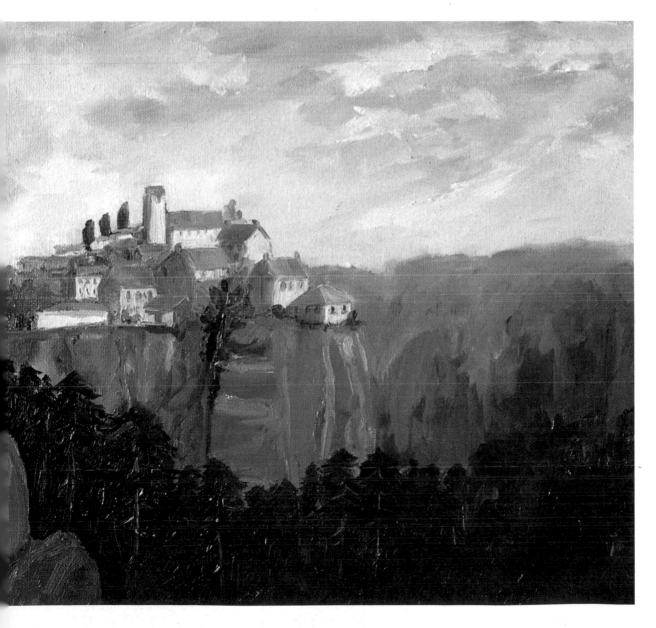

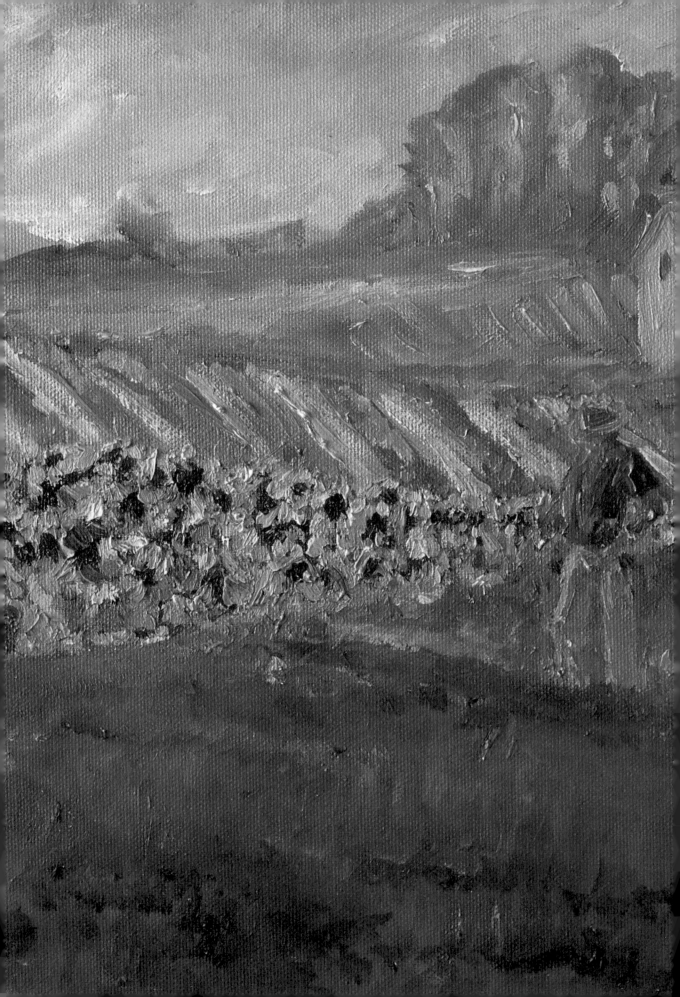

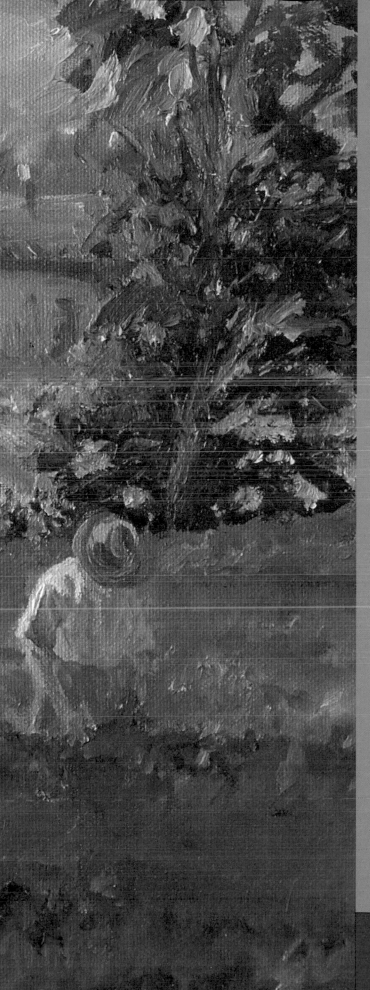

Figures in the Landscape

Adding a few figures into your landscape paintings will bring them to life. Even in the quiet of the countryside it is rare not to see a person in the scene – usually a farmer, or someone out riding a horse. This chapter shows you how to incorporate people successfully into your paintings, particularly – how to paint realistic figures in the middle distance of a landscape.

◀ **Lavender Harvest**
12 x 20 in (31 x 51 cm)

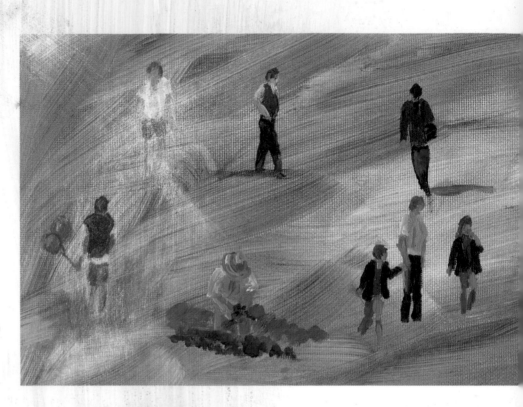

▶ These figures have been painted very simply with merely a few brushstrokes. Paint lots of similar studies to help build confidence.

SIMPLIFYING PEOPLE

Rather than starting with an outline, try to think of people as a series of shapes and brushstrokes. I always start with the body, then add the head, legs, and finally the arms. To avoid worrying about the shape of a nude figure, paint the clothes instead. This way you can build up a reasonable figure shape by painting, fo example, a T-shirt and then long pants, helping to establish the basic figure before adding the arms and the head. I the figure is moving, it is the angle of the torso and of the legs that establishe the stance much more descriptively than the head.

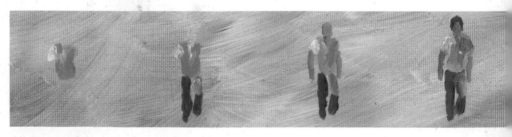

▲ Start with the torso of the figure and use a medium flat brush to paint a basic T-shirt. I have used a very pale blue mixed from white with a little French ultramarine.

▲ Add the pant legs, using French ultramarine darkened with a little cadmium orange.

▲ Mix a flesh tone from cadmium orange, raw sienna, and white to form the head and arms.

▲ Use a little dark bro mixed from light red and French ultramarine, to p the hair. Finish the top o the pants with darkened blue and add a little mor shading to the T-shirt. Th you have it – a simple figure to paint in the middle distance.

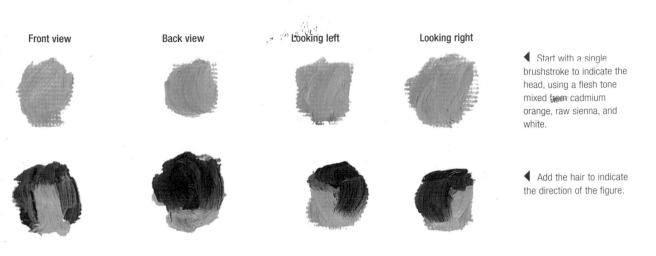

Front view   Back view   Looking left   Looking right

◀ Start with a single brushstroke to indicate the head, using a flesh tone mixed from cadmium orange, raw sienna, and white.

◀ Add the hair to indicate the direction of the figure.

▼ Make lots of quick sketches of children to help atune your eyes to the differences in the scale of proportions between adults and children. This will help make your paintings of children look more realistic.

HEADS AND FACES

When painting figures in the middle distance as part of a landscape or street scene, it is not necessary to paint the details of faces. Details at such a small scale can sometimes make the figure appear rather comical, as can painting feet. Instead, use the angle of the head and the hairline to indicate the direction the figure is facing.

When painting the hair, use only a single brushstroke to avoid picking up any underlying flesh color. Wipe off any unwanted color between each brushstroke as you work.

CHILDREN

When painting children you need to be aware of slightly different proportions. While adults have a head that is about one seventh of the full height, children under twelve have a somewhat different ratio, with the head being approximately one fifth of their full height. Getting the proportions right for children will make them look natural rather than causing

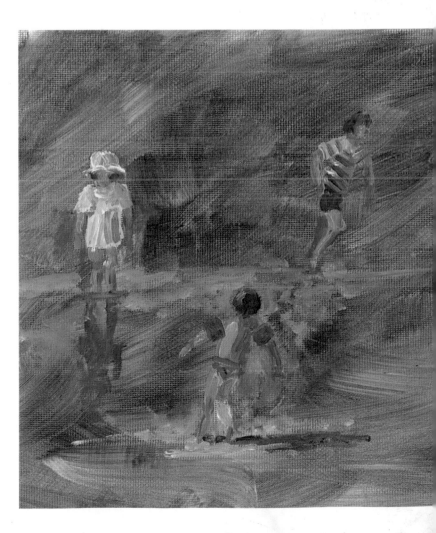

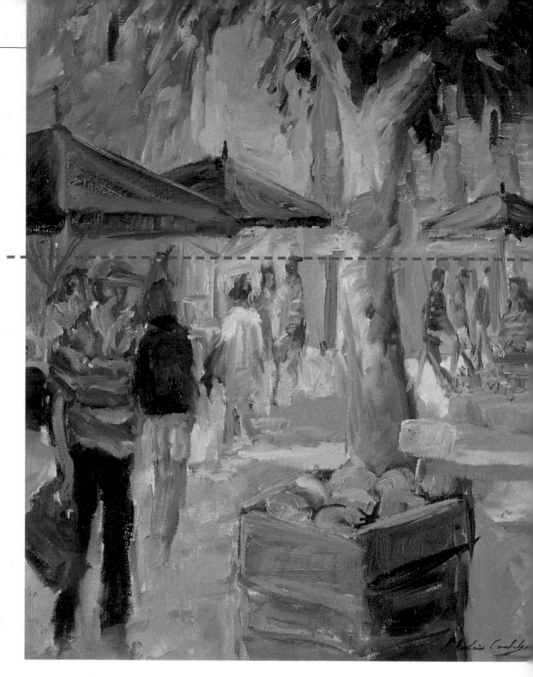

▶ **Melons à Vendre, Bourgeneuf**
18 x 14 in (46 x 36 cm)
When figures are viewed on level ground, the heads will line up across the horizon, as indicated by the dotted line.

tips

◆ *An easy mistake is to paint a figure too large or small for a doorway, so do be aware this.*

◆ *Avoid painting feet since this often makes a figure appear static and rather comical.*

them to appear to be very small adults.

FIGURES IN SCALE

Figures will only look realistic in your paintings if they are in correct proportion both to their surroundings and to other figures in the painting. This is not as complicated as it sounds. If the figures are on level ground, correct perspective shows all the heads of figures more or less lined up. This means in practice that figures nearer the front of the painting will appear larger in size,

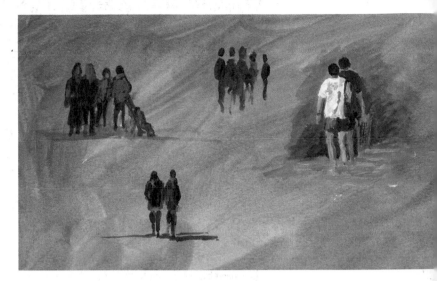

...ut their heads will still be level with ...hose further away and consequently ...maller in size. The painting of *Melons à* ...*Vendre, Bourgeneuf* on page 98 shows this.

SIMPLIFYING GROUPS OF PEOPLE AND PAINTING ANIMALS

...When tackling a group of figures you can ...ometimes paint them as one shape, with ... few added details. Alternately, if you ...aint separate figures standing close to ...ach other, make sure some of them ...verlap. Try to avoid depicting figures ...merely touching each other as this makes ... difficult to see which figure is in front ...f the other.

In the countryside people are often ...ccompanied by a dog, which you will ...want to include. Again, there is no need ...o paint in the fine detail of the animal; ...he key is to capture its movement and ...haracter. Concentrate on getting the ...proportions of the dog right – the size of ...s body compared to its legs, for ...nstance. Make sure that the dog is in ...cale with any figures in the painting.

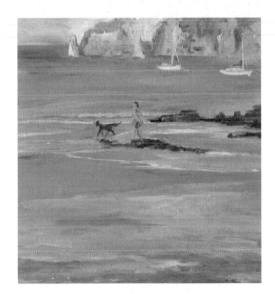

▲ When painting groups of figures look at the overall shape and paint this first, adding the heads afterward. Bee careful when painting figures close together to overlap them so that it is obvious which one is in front of the other.

◀ **Beach Dog**
12 x 12 in (31 x 31 cm)

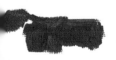

▲ Start with the body, using a ...edium flat brush loaded with ...ght red. Most dogs have a fairly ...ctangular body, with a smallish ...ead.

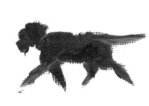

▲ Add the tail and legs using a No. 4 round detail brush. Try to paint the legs with only one brushstroke, and don't worry about adding the feet.

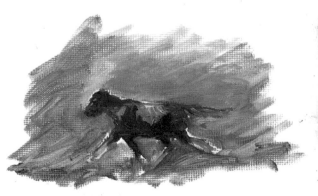

▲ Having established the basic outline of the dog, add some patches of white to define the shape of the body. Use a little French ultramarine to shade under the dog's belly. A touch of white on two of the legs and the nose for highlights finishes the painting.

demonstration
Low Tide, Daymer Bay

The beach is a great place to paint figures. There are usually plenty of people moving around or simply relaxing, making it easy to include them in your paintings. It is helpful to note the key colors of T-shirts, towels, dogs, etc. Most people who visit the beach are will often stay all day, allowing you to settle down in a quiet corner to sketch them before including them in your finished painting.

you will need

canvas size 12 x 18 in (30 x 45 cm)
(primed with acrylic burnt sienna)
brushes: No. 8 short flat, No. 4 short flat, No. 4 round, No. 10 short flat

colors

French ultramarine, light red, cadmium orange, sap green, lemon yellow, raw sienna, cerulean blue, and titanium white

tips

♦ *Use both the flat and sharp edges of the brush to create different textures within the cliff face.*

♦ *Use cadmium orange and white darkened with a little raw sienna for a basic flesh tone.*

♦ *Paint the figures first, before you paint the beach. This enables you to correct mistakes without having to repaint the surrounding beach each time.*

♦ *Check the angles of reflections, especially those of moving figures. Do not forget that the dog has a reflection as well!*

♦ *Vary the tones of the foreground beach to show areas of wet and dry sand.*

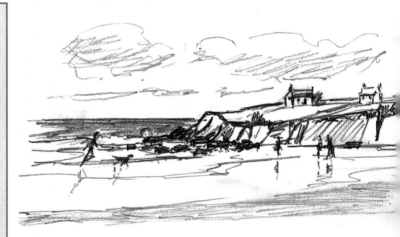

▲ **STEP ONE**

My initial sketch of the beach at Daymer concentrated on the composition with its lo cliff and cottages perched on the edge. As figures moved about on the beach in front o me, I noted their positions relative to my sketch. I then made a few separate figure sketches as well.

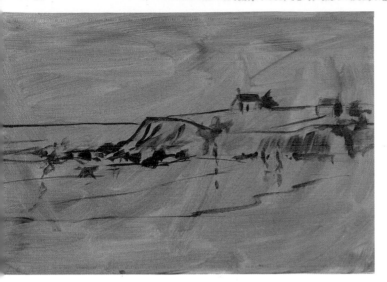

◀ STEP TWO

With so many cool blue shades in this beach scene, using a canvas primed with burnt sienna helps to counteract the coldness and give the finished painting an overall warmth. So, working on a tinted canvas, I established the basic composition with a No. 4 flat brush using French ultramarine. The four figures and the dog are basic shapes in the correct scale – simply a head, body, and a single brushstroke for each leg.

STEP THREE

started painting the background cliffs, using No. 8 flat brush with a mixture of lemon ellow and cerulean blue for the brightest reen, softened with a little raw sienna in laces. The red cliffs were painted with a nixture of light red and French ultramarine or the darker tones, with raw sienna and hite for the lighter areas. Next I blocked in he two cottages, white for the sunlit wall, ith French ultramarine and cadmium range for the shadowed side. The roofs were ne same mixture, but with less white and nore orange.

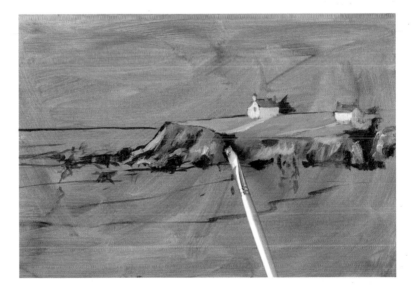

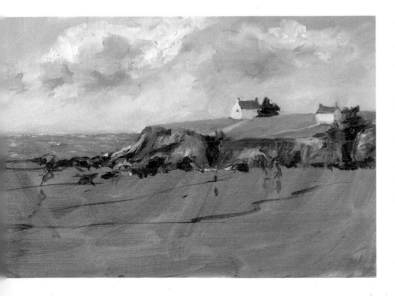

◀ STEP FOUR

After I had finished painting the cliffs I added the shrubs, using sap green and raw sienna. I blocked in the sea to the horizon using a No. 8 flat brush loaded with French ultramarine and cadmium orange, placing flecks of white to give an impression of distant waves. For the sky I chose a No. 10 flat brush. I started with cerulean blue and white at the top, then painted the clouds using cerulean blue and cadmium orange for the shadow side, with white and cadmium orange for the sunlit tops.

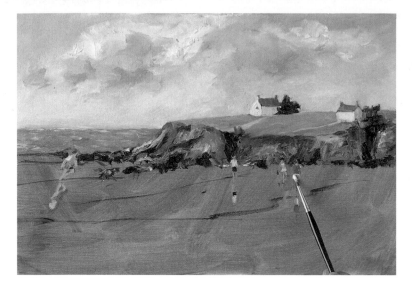

◀ STEP FIVE

It is considerably easier to paint the figures a
this stage, working directly onto the blank
canvas. Mistakes made now can be cleaned
off without damaging any surrounding wet
paint. I used a No. 4 round brush and,
starting with the body in each case, built the
figure, adding head, arms, and legs. Using th
same colors, I painted the reflection at the
same time.

▶ STEP SIX

With the figures now established, I began to
paint the surrounding beach and wave. I used
a No. 8 flat brush as much as possible, but
also a No. 4 round brush. Lemon yellow and
cerulean blue made a good mixture for the
shallow water and the wave as it falls onto
the beach. It is always tempting just to use
pure white where the wave hits the rocks, but
adding a little shadowed area at the base of
the wave gives the breaker more form.

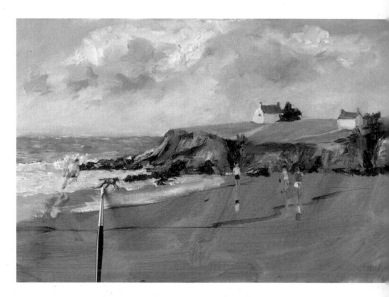

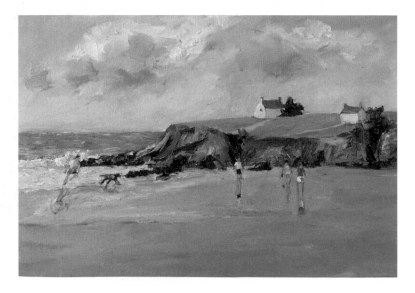

◀ STEP SEVEN

I painted the beach using a No. 8 flat brush
and a basic tone of raw sienna and white, bu
with a little light red added toward the
bottom of the canvas. With very light
pressure on the brush, I added stripes of
cerulean blue and white across this beach
tone to give the impression of water runnin
back toward the sea.

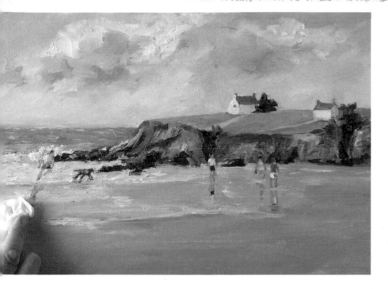

◀ STEP EIGHT

I realized that I had put the reflection of the figure on the far left at the wrong angle, so with a clean rag dipped in a little painting medium, I gently wiped off the paint back to pure canvas. Finally (*see below*), I repainted the reflection and surrounding beach. I added windows to the cottages on the cliff, using French ultramarine and cadmium orange. A few stones on the beach completed the picture.

▼ **Low Tide, Daymer Bay** 12 x 18 in (30 x 45 cm)

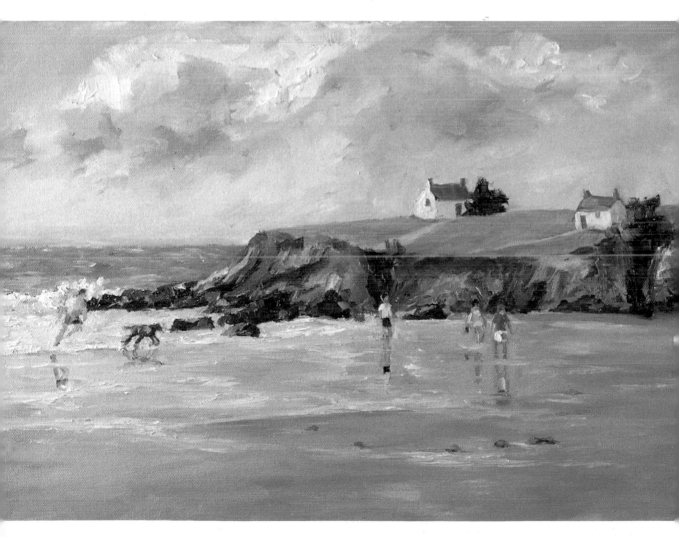

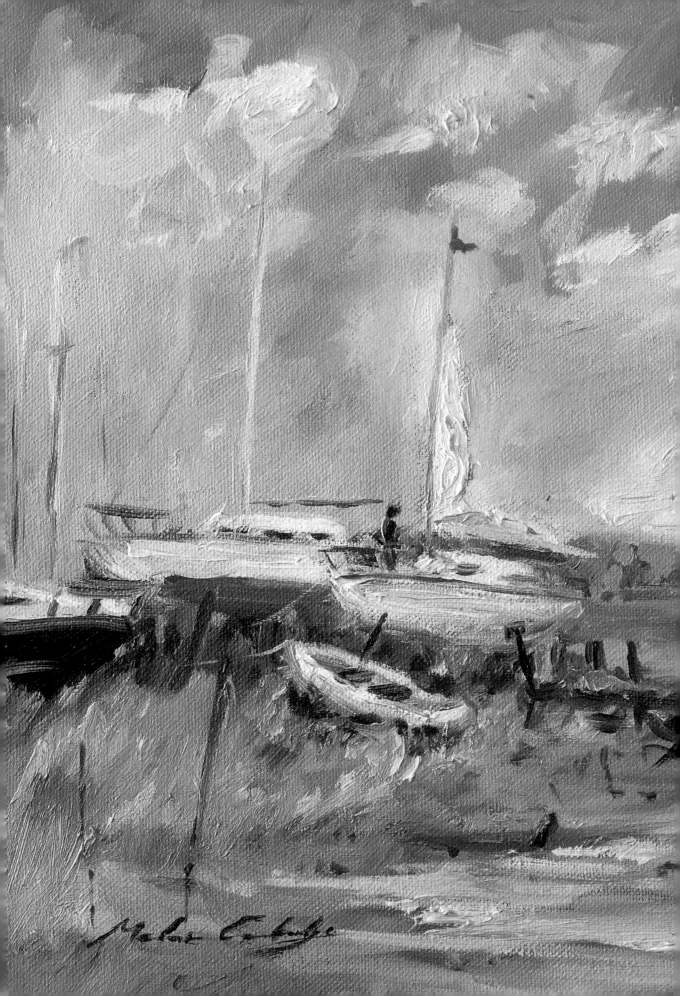

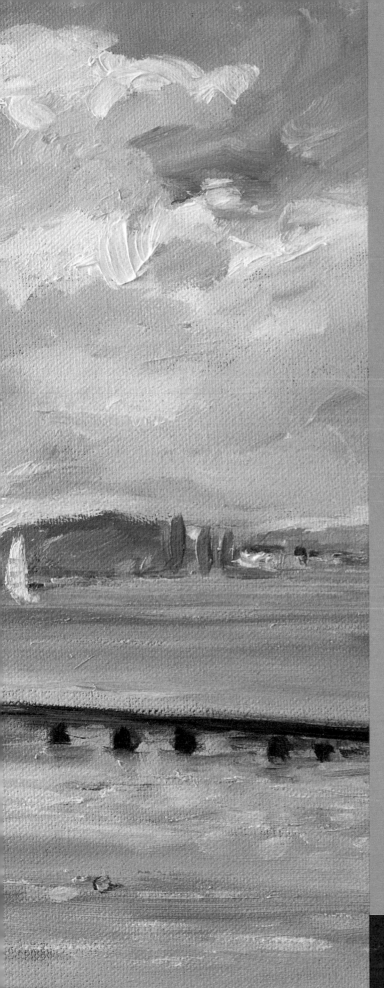

Boats and Harbors

Boats and harbors offer an almost limitless variety of material for the artist, from a single boat moored on a river bank to harbors with fishing boats, yachts, and all the associated equipment of the waterfront. Let us look at each element separately to help you to build up your confidence for painting this subject, giving you the skill to paint a simple boat shape to a full harbor view.

◀ Breezy Afternoon, West Itchenor
10 x 12 in (25 x 31 cm)

LOOKING AT BOATS

When you first begin to look at boats as a subject for painting, you realize just how many different types and shapes there are, so it is very helpful to build up your knowledge by sketching the basic types.

Some students find it difficult to draw the outline shape, so try instead to build the boat shape from the outset by working in paint directly with no pre-drawing. Try to avoid thinking "It's a boat, and I can't draw boats," but treat this subject as a series of block shapes instead. Use a No. 8 flat brush and a No 4 rigger brush to sketch in each shape or surface almost like an abstract pattern. Gradually, as the shapes link together, the overall shape of the boat will begin to appear.

The example here of using paint to 'build' a basic yacht seen from the side shows you how to simplify a complex subject, like a boat, down to abstract shapes. The details are added toward the end. This alternate approach to painting should make it much easier to tackle more complicated subjects at an early stage in your artistic development without the fear of having to produce an accurate drawing before you start.

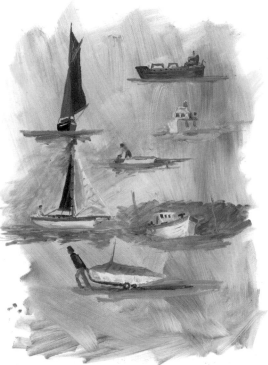

▶ Fill your sketchbook with as many different boats as you can for reference.

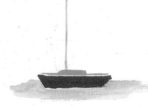

▲ Use a No. 4 flat brush loaded with alizarin crimson to paint the hull, ideally using only three or four brushstrokes.

▲ Mix French ultramarine and cadmium orange with white for a mid-gray shade and use this to paint the flat shape of the yacht's topsides with a No. 4 round detail brush. Then mix yellow ocher and white for the mast. A simple, single line is enough.

▲ Mark in the yacht's window by darkening the gray with a little more French ultramarine. Paint the rolled up sail as a long stripe and add a spot of the mast color at the end.

▲ Details are added in white — the rail at the front of the yacht and two fenders (painted directly into the wet red of the hull). Using the mast color, add a series of lines to the sail to indicate the ties and, finally, indicate the stripe along the lower part of the hull with a little pure French ultramarine.

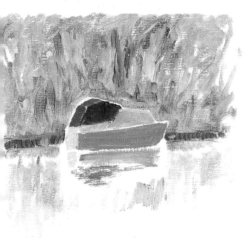

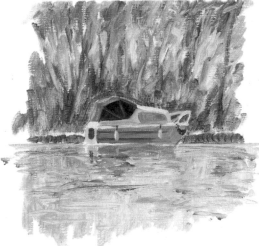

◀ River cruiser
The hull shape is a darkish tone, and the back of the boat is painted white. The shape for the topsides is in a lighter tone. The canvas cover is two flat shapes, in dark and light tones. Stripes are indicated on the side of the cover using the paler tone. The window is painted and then the frame, and a white rail is painted on the front. A dark area is painted into the back of the hull. Two laths on the hull sides are worked directly into the wet paint underneath and a curved fender shape is added to the front. Finally, two fenders are painted on the sides using white paint.

DIFFERENT TYPES OF BOATS

Now, let us consider some other types of boats. An example of a river cruiser and a fishing boat are shown here. Notice how in the example of the river cruiser the boat's overall shape – its outline – is complete without having done any drawing, but adding the details turns the fairly flat shapes into a finished boat.

Similarly the fishing boat starts out as a series of blocks, but because it has two colors in the hull, two separate block shapes combine to give its outline. Details of the rigging are suggested rather than precisely painted, keeping the overall effect loose and lively.

Fishing boats seem to have an enormous amount of complex apparatus, but keep these details to a minimum to prevent them becoming too dominant in the painting. The finished result appears quite detailed, but these details are quite roughly painted using lively brushstrokes that keep the picture spontaneous.

tips

◆ To help build up your confidence, sketch boats using a brush or thick marker pen that will enable you to use blocks rather than lines from the outset.

◆ When viewing boats from ground that is level with the water, there is not much distance between the boats and the far bank or horizon. Place your boats high up toward the horizon for a realistic effect.

◀ Fishing boat
Start with the hull, painting the top section and keel as stripes. The boat is at a slight angle, so the stripes appear narrower toward the back. The cabin is a cube shape. Cabin windows are single brushstrokes and fishing floats are simple ball shapes. Other details are indicated sketchily.

▶ **Vieux Port, Honfleur**
10 x 12 in (25 x 31 cm)
This view of Honfleur in
France was painted in my
studio using the photograph
below.

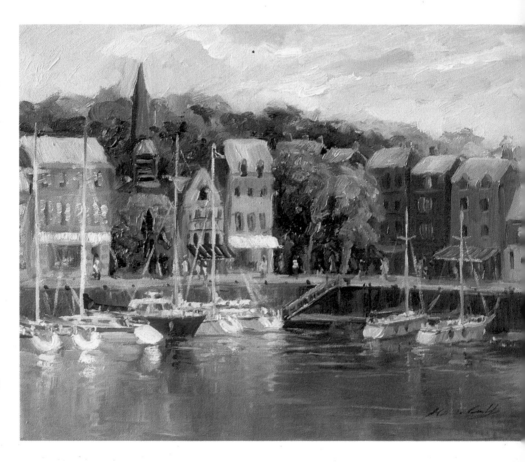

▼ Many of the details in
this photograph have been
simplified in the painting,
especially the buildings in
the background; including
all the details would bring
the buildings too far forward
in the finished painting.
Highlights are strongest on
the foreground yachts and
on the shop canopies.

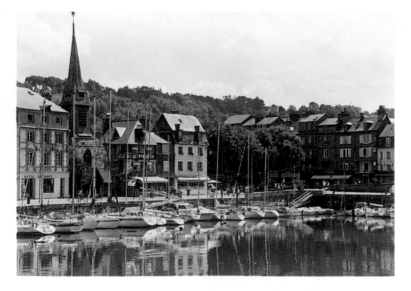

LOOKING AT HARBORS

Harbors are full of activity, fishing
equipment, cranes, buildings, and, of
course, lots of boats. Painting on location
at a harbor can be quite a challenge, so it
is useful to start off by working from
photographs. Ideally, these should be
photographs you have taken yourself or
at least of a place you have visited so that
you are familiar with the scene.

COPING WITH THE DETAILS

Since harbors are such busy places it is
essential to create this feeling of activity
and clutter within your painting. This
can mean including many unusual items
such as cranes, fishing nets, lobster pots
and packing crates as well as buildings
and, of course, people.

A first visit to a busy harbor can be a
rather intimidating experience for the
amateur artist. There seems to be so
much; but do not panic! There is no need
to paint everything you see; just try to

create an atmosphere of paraphernalia and busy movement. Treat all of the items in the same way as the boats themselves, as abstract shapes to begin with, then adding a few extra details to bring them to life.

Look carefully at the sketch on the right and you will see how each item has been simplified – most of the details of ropes and lines have been left out on complex equipment such as the crane. Fishing nets are simply suggested using a criss-cross pattern, while the floats are simple ball shapes with a loop on top.

Wherever there are boats and moorings there are usually people, working on the boats or simply walking along the waterfront. Adding a few simple figures, even in the background, helps to bring seaside paintings to life. Painting figures is covered on pages

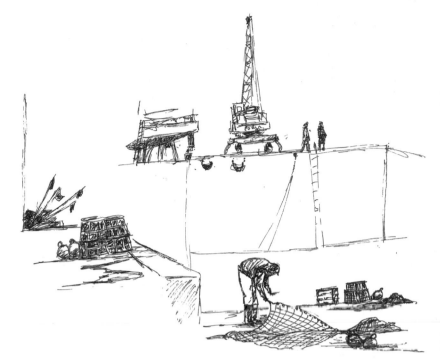

94–103, but here are a few more ideas when relating them specifically to harbor scenes. Copy these simple studies if you wish before collecting your own ideas from sketches or photographs.

▲ A quick study of cranes, packing cases, nets, and floats.

◀ Whenever you see people working near boats, make a few rapid sketches. Try to capture their movements and actions.

demonstration
Oyster Boats, Ile de Ré

For this scene of fishing boats near La Rochelle in France, I decided to work on a background of alizarin crimson. The strong turquoise water in particular works well with the cool pink underpainting. I was attracted to the scene by the contrast of turquoise water against the white fishing shack and boats and the fact that the colors were so different from the soft tones of an English landscape.

you will need

canvas size: 10 x 12 in (25 x 30 cm)
(primed with acrylic alizarin crimson)
brushes: No. 8 short flat, No. 4 short flat, No. 4 round, No. 4 rigger, No. 10 short flat

colors

French ultramarine, light red, cadmium orange, sap green, lemon yellow, raw sienna, cerulean blue, alizarin crimson, viridian and titanium white.

tips

• *Work with thinned oil color when painting the sky to allow a little of the pink underpainting to show through, giving the sky an overall warm glow.*

• *Try to see only the main block shapes within each boat when you start to paint them. Do not think about details at the initial stage.*

• *Make sure that the mast and the poles of the foreground jetty are all tall enough to break through the horizon line and into the sky.*

• *When adding the ripples to the water, use very light pressure on the brush to produce very fine lines.*

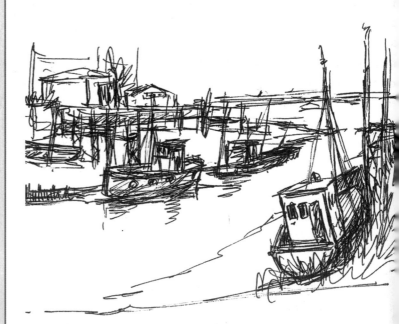

▲ **STEP ONE**
My sketch for this painting shows the basic composition and structure of the fishing boats. Notes alongside it reminded me of the key colors – strong turquoise water, predominantly white boats on the far side of the inlet, and a dark green foreground boat.

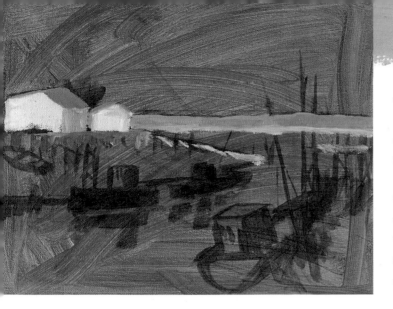

◀ STEP TWO

Having primed the canvas with a thin wash of acrylic alizarin crimson, I blocked in the main shapes with a No. 4 flat brush and French ultramarine. The distant horizon was then painted using French ultramarine, cadmium orange, and white. I used pure white to paint the sunlit sides of the fishing shacks, adding a little French ultramarine and cadmium orange for the shadowed sides.

STEP THREE

hen I painted the trees alongside the fishing hacks, using viridian and raw sienna. With he horizon line established, I painted in the ky using a No. 10 flat brush, with a mixture f cerulean blue and white. This was done by arting at the top of the canvas with the rongest blue tone and adding more white nd a little alizarin crimson toward the orizon. Fast, scrubby brushstrokes created a ense of movement within the sky without he need to paint clearly defined clouds.

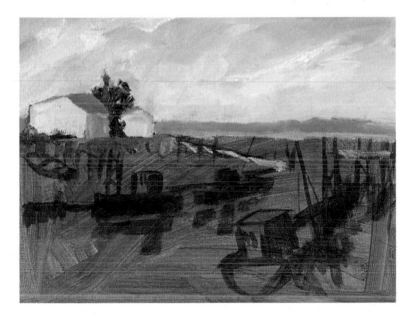

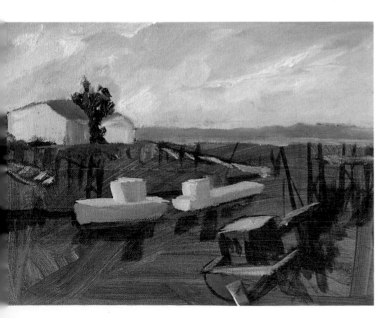

◀ STEP FOUR

Now, to paint the boats. I started with simple block shapes for the two smaller boats, using a No. 4 flat brush and pure white paint for the highlights, adding French ultramarine and cadmium orange for the shadowed sides. The foreground boat was treated in exactly the same way, only the shapes are different. I mixed a basic green shade for the hull using viridian, cadmium orange, and white.

▶ **STEP FIVE**

Still working with the No. 4 flat brush, I used the gray shadow tone to paint in reflected block shapes for the two boats in the middle, using downward brushstrokes only. Next I painted the mud bank with raw sienna, cadmium orange, and white with a No. 8 flat brush. The foreground grassy bank was produced with sap green, light red, and raw sienna, adding in the jetty poles.

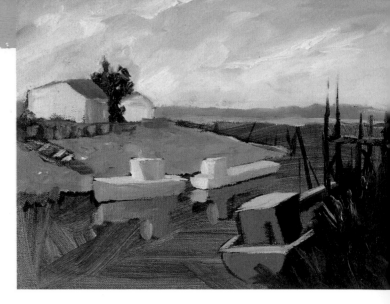

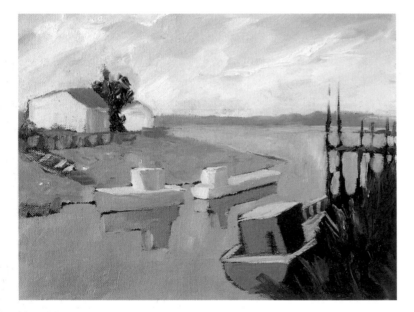

◀ **STEP SIX**

Now for the water. I mixed cerulean blue and a little lemon yellow with white. Using the No. 8 flat brush as much as possible, I painted the whole area of the water, changing to a No. 4 flat brush to paint in between the jetty poles. I produced this flat area of color using downward brushstrokes only. All the surface ripples would be added later on.

▶ **STEP SEVEN**

At last, I could start to add some details. Using a No. 4 rigger brush with light red and French ultramarine, I started to paint in the jetty and poles on the far bank as well as re-stating those in the foreground. Using a No. 4 round brush, I painted the door on the main fishing shack with cerulean blue. On the middle boats I painted one cabin with cerulean blue and the other with viridian and mixed a gray tone using French ultramarine, cadmium orange, and white for the windows. Each boat has a stripe along the top edge of the hull and gray fenders hanging down the side.

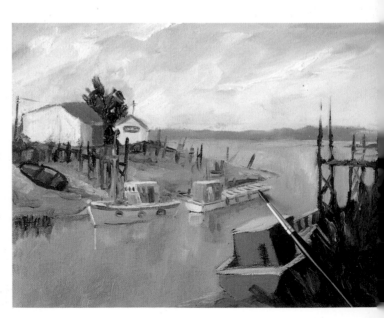

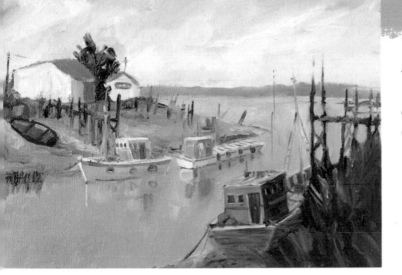

◀ **STEP EIGHT**

I painted the foreground fishing boat in exactly the same way. Now the surface ripples could be added to the water. These were produced with a No. 4 round brush with a little cerulean blue and white gently dragged in horizontal lines over the wet surface. Finally (*see below*), I added two yachts sailing close to the far horizon.

▼ **Oyster Boats, Ile de Ré** 10 x 12 in (25 x 30 cm)

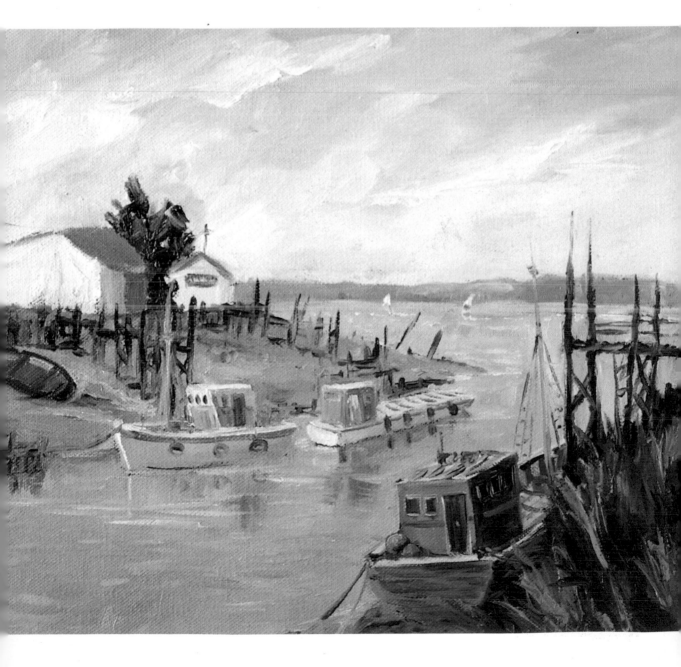

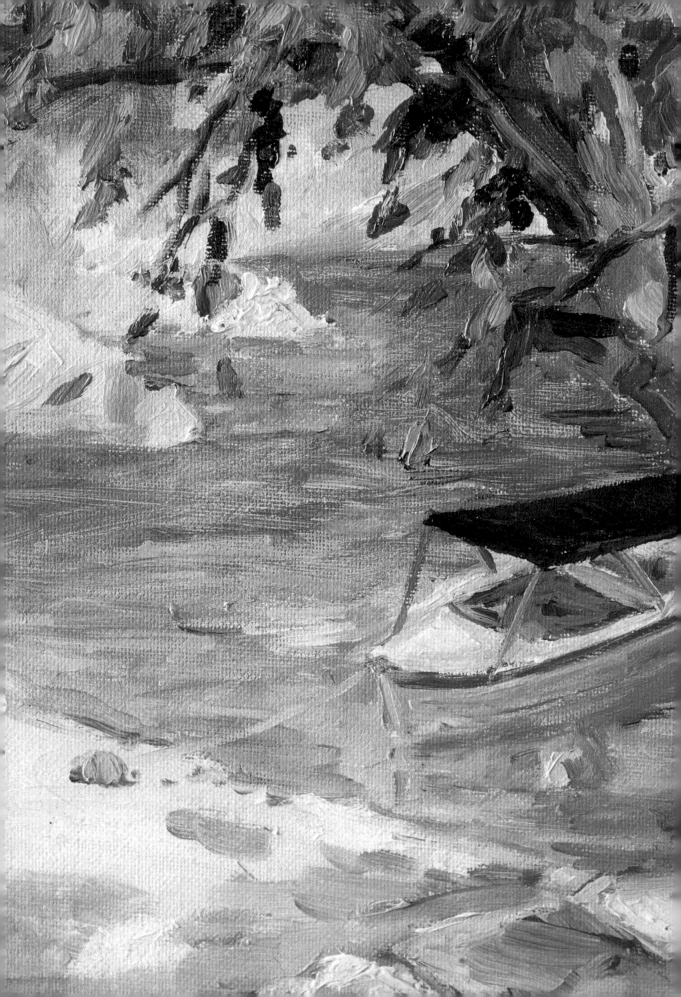

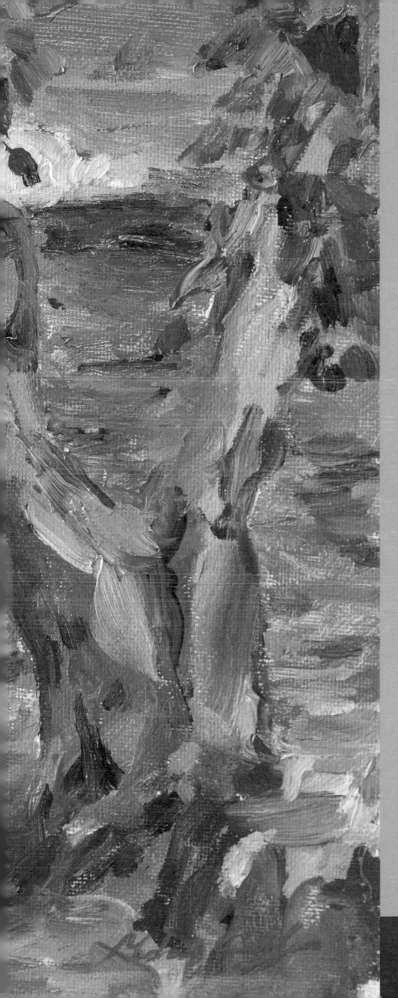

Painting on Location

Trying to capture the many moods of the landscape, from the warmth of a summer's day, through the wonderful colors of autumn, to the bright chill of the first snowfall – these are the elements that excite me about painting outdoors. I hope to dispel any concerns about changing conditions and queries about necessary equipment so that you can enjoy painting outdoors as much as I do.

◀ Paradise Beach, Meganissi
10 x 12 in (25 x 31 cm)

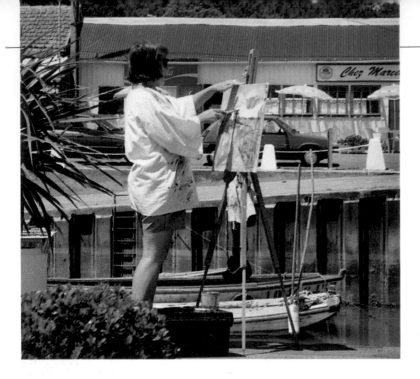

▲ Melanie Cambridge painting on location, France.

▼ **Across the Kentish Weald**
10 x 12 in (25 x 31 cm)
It started to rain heavily, so having blocked in the main areas of the picture, I finished this painting in the studio.

ESSENTIAL EQUIPMENT
Many students claim they cannot possibly paint outdoors because they need so much equipment that it is far too heavy to carry. Here is how to avoid being weighed down when taking oil paints out on location.

If possible, use a pochade box. This will enable you to carry enough paint tubes, necessary brushes, a wet palette, and a small canvas board all in one box.

Do not take any turpentine, just a small bottle of alkyd medium and a few rags. Oil brushes do not dry out immediately, so they can easily wait until the evening back in the studio to be properly cleaned. Simply wiping off excess paint will be fine while you are outside working.

If you take an easel, make sure it is a lightweight wooden sketching easel rather than a metal one. On breezy days you can always tie the easel down with a stone or a log; it is useful to have already attached a piece of cord to the easel for this purpose.

Canvas boards are ideal for use outdoors. Being solid, light cannot shine through from the back. If you wish to use a stretched canvas, place cardboard behind it to cut out any backlighting.

COPING WITH THE ELEMENTS
Even on warm, sunny days if you are sitting still for a couple of hours or so, it is very easy to start to feel cold, and once a chill starts to set in, any hope of a successful painting is usually over for the day. Probably the best solution for outdoor painting is to wear several layers of clothing, including a waterproof top layer and a windbreaker to keep out the draft. Obviously, a hat is another important item; in summer a straw one or at least something with a large peak to keep the sun out of your eyes is useful,

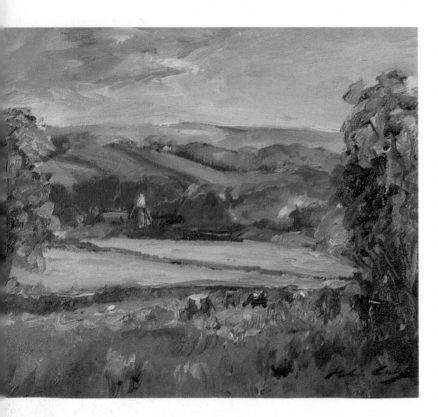

while in winter you will need a hat that keeps your ears warm.

Other items always in my paintbox are sunscreen, insect repellent, and a sting-relief spray for insect bites.

SETTING A TIMESCALE

Light conditions change constantly outdoors. The sun moves considerably in two to three hours, so try to complete each painting within a two-hour time period. This need not be as intimidating as it first seems. To start with, work on a small scale, say 10 x 8 in (25 x 20 cm), and concentrate on getting the key elements of the painting down immediately. Mark in all the shadows and highlights at a very early stage and stick to these, even though they will move as the sun moves across the sky. If there is a complicated building, make a sketch of it, noting positions of windows, details of chimneys, etc. Even take a photograph if this will help you. Details can always be added in the studio, leaving time on location to block in the main areas while light conditions remain constant.

WORKING IN A BUSY LOCATION

Working in a busy location can bring its own problems. Few artists enjoy being surrounded by curious onlookers because this can break up your concentration and often results in a disappointing painting.

Sitting with your back to a wall should prevent people from standing behind you, although this will not stop people from talking. Some artists choose simply to ignore any conversation, making the occasional grunt, but really not answering. You may find it more effective to respond to questions, however, then politely say "If you don't mind, I need to concentrate on this section." Most onlookers are merely interested and will be happy to leave you alone to work rather than upset your concentration, particularly if they are politely asked. The only other solution is to keep away from busy places!

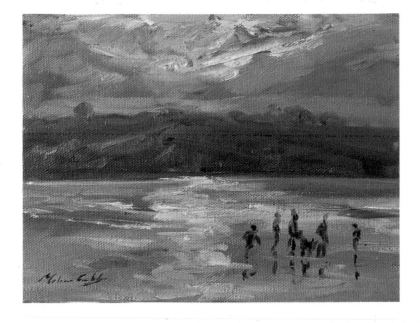

▲ **Sunset, Daymer Bay**
5 x 7 in (13 x 18 cm)
This sunset was painted on location in half an hour using a 6 x 8 in (15 x 20 cm) canvas. Details are very loose, and the foreground figures have been reduced to simple silhouettes.

▼ **Camel Estuary**
5 x 7 in (13 x 18 cm)
Painted looking into the light, details were lost, but the highlights on the bridge and distant hills give this picture a great deal of atmosphere.

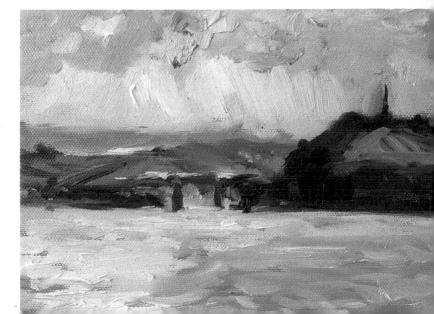

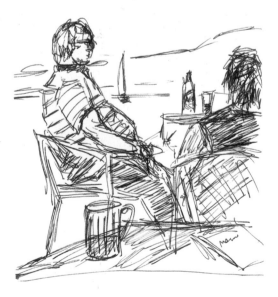

▶ **Tuscan Villa**
12 x 16 in (31 x 41 cm)
When working with unfamiliar landscapes, you may find that the light and colors are very different from your usual palette, so take time to make observations before you start painting.

TRAVELING ABROAD

Taking oil paints with you on trips abroad presents its own problems, particularly if you are traveling by air. Obviously it is not possible to take flammable liquids such as turpentine or kerosene onto an airplane, or to transport wet oil paintings in a suitcase. One solution is to use fast-drying alkyd oils and medium. Not only can these be taken onto planes (though not as hand baggage), but when used on their own they will dry within one or two days. Instead of trying to buy kerosene when arriving at your destination, take a can of soap cleaner. This is often sold as brush restorer for acrylics, but it cleans oils from brushes just as effectively. You simply wet the surface of the soap and work the bristles into it and then rinse with water.

SELECTING YOUR SPOT

When you arrive at a new location, the choice of subject matter can be amazing. Spend the first day wandering around, taking in the sights and atmosphere. Make quick sketches of whatever catches your eye, from a simple doorway to figures at a café table or a view of a distant hilltop. It is a good idea not to take a camera on the first day since it can be tempting to simply take lots of photographs and not do any sketching. Although photographs are useful for general reference material, rapid sketches with a few scribbled color notes often bring back more accurate and personal memories of a scene.

▶ As well as enjoying painting on location, try to find time to sketch, even if the results are as rough as this one — produced while waiting for the ferry!

Having found a suitable spot to set up your painting, preferably in the shade and with your back to a wall to avoid too many interruptions, spend a few moments assessing the scene in front of you. Colors may be stronger than you are used to. Sunlight can bleach out pavements and stonework to almost pure white. In hotter climates you may prefer to work on a white canvas to keep the colors pure. Alternately, alizarin crimson makes a cooler undertone, so it is a matter of experimenting to find what works best for you.

Work on a small scale and try to produce a morning and afternoon painting. Concentrate on blocking in the main shapes and establishing areas of light and shade. Make notes of any special details in your sketchbook and take a few photographs as extra reference material before you leave.

BACK AT THE STUDIO

When you return from a painting trip, put all of your paintings to one side to look at again in two or three days' time. This helps you to avoid feelings of disappointment. I often find that if I look critically at my work as soon as I return to the studio, with the outdoor image still fresh in my mind, I feel disappointed with the results. This is because I am not looking at the painting as a painting, but instead judging it against the outdoor scene. After a couple of days it becomes easier to consider the paintings critically in their own right, so that is the time to consider making any minor changes or improvements.

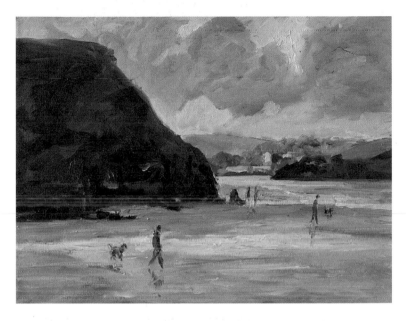

▼ **Daymer Bay, Cornwall – as painted on location**
12 x 16 in (30 x 41 cm)
Painted in just over one hour on a cold, clear afternoon in December.

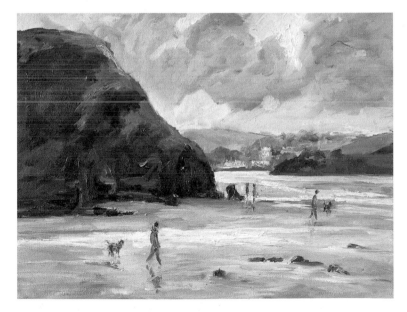

▲ **Daymer Bay, Cornwall – back at the studio**
12 x 16 in (30 x 41 cm)
Highlights to the foreground cliff helped to give it more shape, while extra stones on the beach lead the eye into the painting.

demonstration
Morning Light, Kefallonia

The village of Assos nestles at the bottom of a steep cliff on the Greek Island of Kefallonia and makes an enticing subject in clear morning light. Having settled on a stone wall at the end of the quay, I decided to use the steep hillside as a backdrop rather than looking out to sea. The light was strong, even early in the morning, so I chose to paint directly onto white canvas to keep the colors cooler.

you will need

canvas 14 x 16 in (35 x 40 cm)
brushes: No. 8 short flat, No. 4 short flat, No. 4 round, No. 10 short flat

colors

French ultramarine, cadmium orange, yellow ocher, viridian, cerulean blue, sap green, lemon yellow, light red, alizarin crimson, and titanium white.

tips

◆ Keep the brushstrokes fluid to create the effect of woodland rather than individual tree shapes.

◆ Use angled brushmarks to give a three-dimensional shape to the olive trees.

◆ Use light pressure on the brush for the reflections in the water to avoid muddying the paint underneath.

◆ Adding stripes to the fisherman's top helps to make him look more three-dimensional.

◆ Keep the details simple for the windows in the buildings on the hillside to maintain a sense of depth.

◆ Darken the foreground shadows to make the sunlit quay appear brighter.

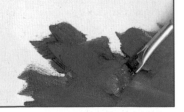

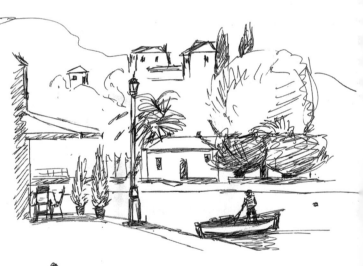

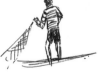

▲ **STEP ONE**

Before starting to paint I made a sketch of the scene and a separate note of the fisherman sorting his nets. Working on location can present problems for the artist; figures tend to come and go and there was also the chance that the boat I hoped to make the center of interest would move out to sea before I had finished painting it.

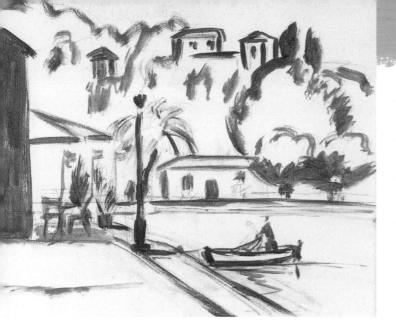

◀ **STEP TWO**

Putting the sketch to one side, I blocked in the scene with a No. 4 flat brush using French ultramarine. The shadowed side of the café is a solid blue, and the shadow underneath the café awning was also designated in blue at this stage.

STEP THREE

Using the No. 8 flat brush, I began to block in the background hillside. I started at the top of the canvas, mixing viridian, cerulean blue, and white for the pale mint green shades. Yellow ocher was added to this mixture for warmer green tones lower down. I left the four middle-ground trees at this stage.

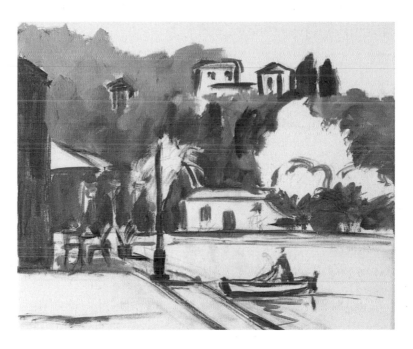

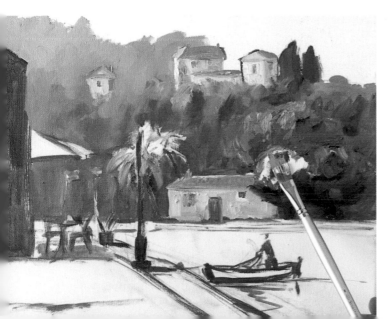

◀ **STEP FOUR**

Switching to a No 4 flat brush, I blocked in the buildings on the far side of the bay with a mixture of yellow ocher, cerulean blue, and white, with cadmium orange and cerulean blue for the roofs. Windows were marked in with a No. 4 round brush, using French ultramarine and cadmium orange. Using a No. 8 flat brush, I painted the large tree on the right-hand side with sap green and yellow ocher, while the olive trees in front are a mixture of viridian and cadmium orange.

▶ **STEP FIVE**

A No. 10 flat brush loaded with cerulean blue and white was used for the water. I started just beneath the middle building, using flat brushstrokes first of all. Then I held the brush flat against the canvas, dragging it gently over the surface to paint the ripples. More cerulean blue and a very little lemon yellow was added to the mixture as I worked toward the bottom of the canvas.

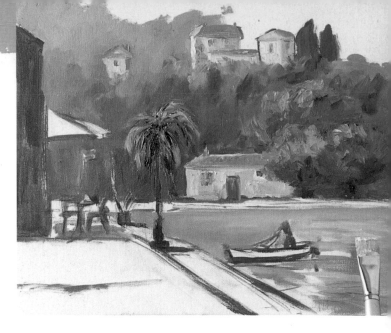

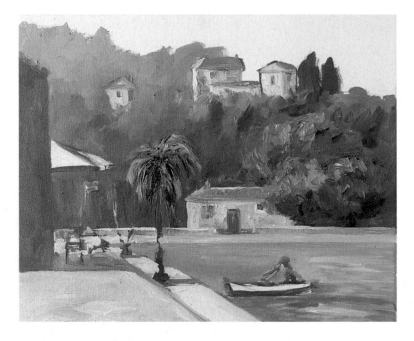

◀ **STEP SIX**

When the water was finished, I linked the fa edge of the water to the shore by painting th shallow beach using yellow ocher and white. The low wall that divides the beach from the village was painted in soft gray tones mixed from cerulean blue, cadmium orange, and white. I blocked in the side of the café with a No. 10 flat brush using light red, French ultramarine, and white. The sunlit foreground was produced from cadmium orange and cerulean blue with plenty of white added. Then I used a darker version of the same mixture for the shadow under the café awning and along the edge of the quay.

▶ **STEP SEVEN**

Using the No. 10 flat brush, I painted the sky with cerulean blue, cadmium orange, and white. The café awning is white along the top highlight, but I painted the shadow with light red and French ultramarine with plenty of white. The same gray, but much stronger, was used to paint the lamppost. The café chairs are cerulean blue, painted directly over the wet pavement shadow. Underlying gray tones picked up by the No. 4 round brush soften the colors of the chairs.

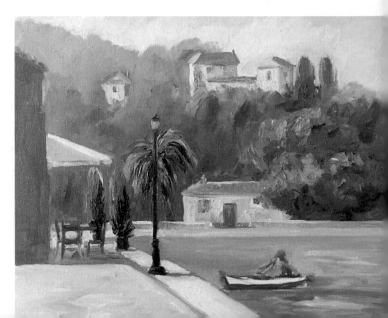

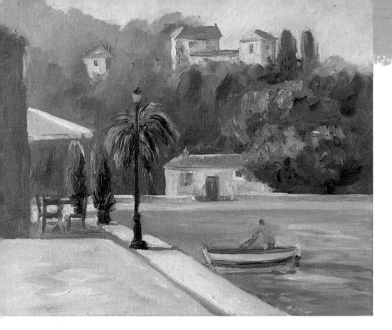

◀ STEP EIGHT

I painted the boat hull in horizontal stripes. I also blocked in the fisherman, painting his top and shorts, then adding arms, legs, and head. A few horizontal reflections were added beneath the boat. Finally (*see below*), I added red stripes to the fisherman's sweater, and I repainted the café chairs, which appeared too large in proportion to the rest of the painting.

▼ **Morning Light, Kefallonia** 14 x 16 in (35 x 40 cm)

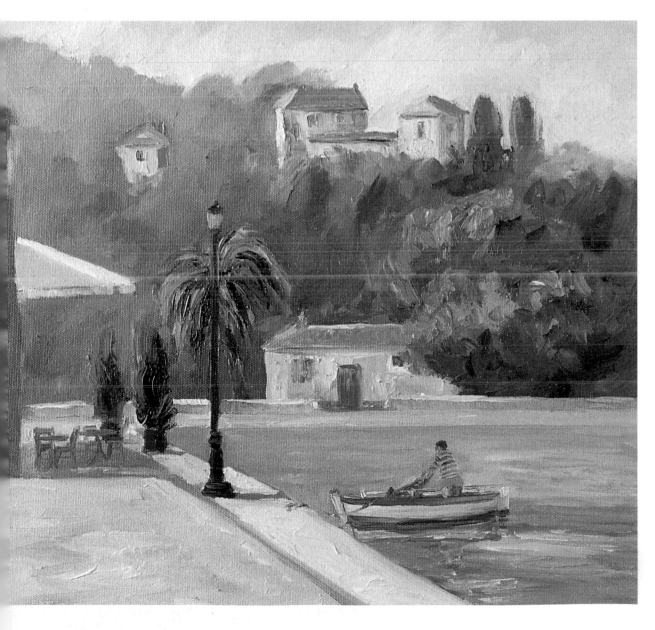

Finishing Touches

After a painting is completely dry, usually after about a month, it should be varnished. I recommend just one coat of retouching varnish, applied with a soft brush. As oil paint dries, dull patches can appear on the surface, caused by some of the paint sinking into the canvas. By varnishing your paintings these dull patches are covered over. The varnish also brings back to life those darker areas in which some of the subtle changes in tones may have been lost. Try it and see; you will be surprised just how much better your painting appears after it has been varnished. To show off your finished painting to its best advantage, it needs to be framed. Unlike watercolors, oil paintings are not usually framed under glass, so the frame itself tends to be somewhat larger. Even for a small painting, say 10 x 12 in (25 x 30 cm), I prefer to use at least a 2 in (5 cm) wide frame, with an inner slip molding. An inner slip molding provides a visual breathing space between the painting and the frame (rather like a mattt does for watercolors). The frame itself should complement the colors of the painting rather than being too dominant.

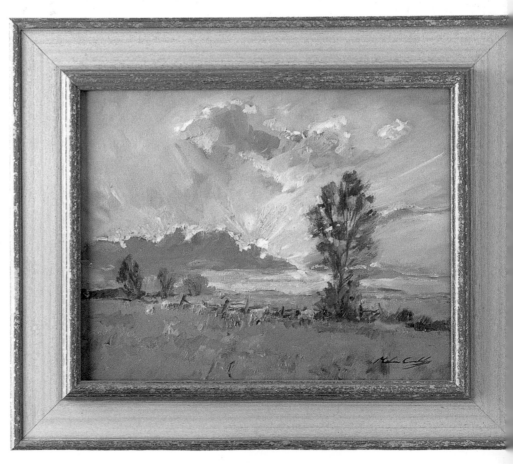

▶ **Sunset over Romney Marsh**
11 x 14 in (28 x 36 cm)
Smaller paintings can often look very good in a large frame. This one is
2 in (5 cm) wide.

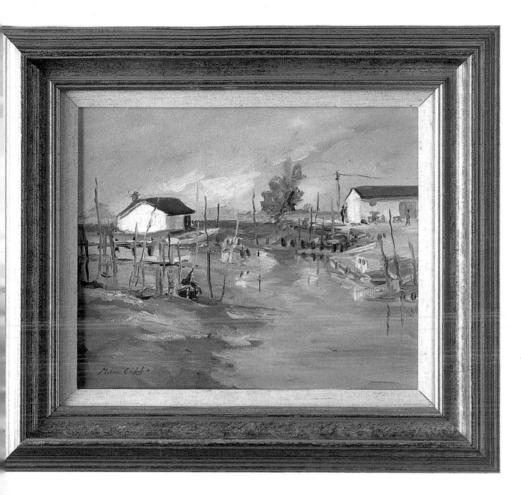

◀ **Fishing Huts, Ile de Ré**
10 x 12 in (25 x 30 cm)
Using an inner slip frame
provides a separation line
between the frame and the
painting. The sloping shape
of the frame also helps to
guide the viewer's eye
toward the painting.

XHIBITING YOUR WORK

ost artists want to exhibit their work
om time to time. For the first-time
hibitor the opportunity can often be
rough a local art society, most of which
ld annual member exhibitions. The
ore ambitious might consider submitting
ork to various open-juried exhibitions
d competitions run by colleges and
ajor art organizations. These exhibitions
ovide an excellent indication of an
tist's progress and give the novice
mething to aim for. The selection process
very severe, however; having a piece
cepted is an achievement in itself.

Most commercial galleries are happy to
ok at new work, but it is courteous to
ake an appointment. It is worth visiting
any potential galleries beforehand both to
check the type of work on display to see
whether the quality and style of your work
fit in with the gallery's image. Getting your
paintings accepted at a gallery is difficult,
however; you need self confidence to cope
with rejection time and again.

Another way to present your work to
the public is by taking part in one of the
many art fairs around the country. Usually
space is limited, and you will need to
book a spot in advance. The thrill of
having your own work on display as well
as meeting and talking to people who are
interested in your work is a great boost to
morale.   If you sell a painting at the fair,
then all the hard work and preparation
are suddenly worthwhile!

Jargon Buster

ALLA PRIMA   Meaning 'at the first.' Used to describe an oil painting produced in one painting session, worked entirely wet-in-wet.

BODY COLOR   Describes any color when mixed with white. Adding white changes the paint's characteristics slightly, making it more opaque (*far right*).

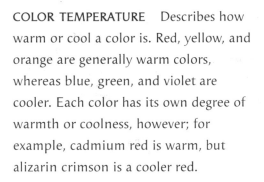

COLOR TEMPERATURE   Describes how warm or cool a color is. Red, yellow, and orange are generally warm colors, whereas blue, green, and violet are cooler. Each color has its own degree of warmth or coolness, however; for example, cadmium red is warm, but alizarin crimson is a cooler red.

COMPLEMENTARY COLORS   Each complementary color is created by mixing the two other primaries together. For example: red's complementary is green (that is, blue and yellow mixed together). Similarly, blue's complementary is orange; the complementary of yellow is purple.

EN PLEIN AIR   Describes a painting produced 'in the open air' (that is, painted outdoors on location).

'FAT OVER LEAN'   When painting with a traditional oil and turpentine medium it is necessary to start with a mainly turpentine-based medium and gradually add more oil as the painting progresses. This is to prevent cracking of the later layers of oil paint (see 'oiling out'). Lean refers to the thin turpentine-based medium; Fat refers to the thicker, more oily medium that is applied later – never the other way round. Using an alkyd medium rather than mixing your own avoids this potential difficulty.

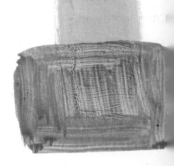

GLAZING   Thin layers of paint applied over an already dry oil painting. Colors may be mixed with retouching varnish create a translucent layer. Glazes are a useful method of unifying a badly colored painting or enhancing one particular area.

...OUND   The surface on which the
...inting is actually made. Often a toned
...colored ground is applied on top of
...e initial primer coat, using raw sienna
...another earth color thinned to a
...sh-like consistency with turpentine.

...CAL COLOR   This is the true color of
...object: for example, a blue ball or red
...vel. This local color, however, is
...ected both by light and its
...rroundings. A blue ball lit by a bright
...otlight, although actually blue all over,
...pears much lighter where the spotlight
...ches the top and similarly much
...ker on the shadow side. The local
...or, blue, is changed by the light. These
...ter and darker
...as are
...wn as
... tonal
...or.

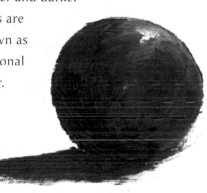

...HLSTICK   A fairly long stick with a
...her- or cloth-covered knob at one
...l, used to steady the wrist while
...nting details.

...DIUM   Traditionally this referred to
...paint itself. However, the term is also
...d to describe the thinning liquid or
...mixed with oil paint to thin and
...d colors together.

OILING OUT   As oil paint dries out
underlying layers can pull oil from the
top layer of paint, causing the surface to
crack. Wiping a thin layer of linseed oil
onto the surface of a touch-dry painting
(with a cotton ball or a soft brush) feeds
the top surface of paint and protects it
from cracking.

PRIMER   The initial coat applied to raw
canvas to create a suitable painting
surface. This may be a gesso primer or a
modern acrylic primer. It is also possible
to use household emulsion on hardboard
or wood to create a suitable surface for
oil paint.

TONAL KEY   Generally used to describe
the overall lightness or darkness of a
painting. For example, a bright beach
scene full of light and bright colors
would be regarded as 'high key,' whereas
a soft evening landscape might be
termed 'low key.'

TONKING   Placing newsprint over the
wet surface of a painting in order to
remove the top layer of paint. Press
down gently on the paper and then peel
back. This technique was popular with
the Impressionists.

Index Page numbers in *italic* refer to captions